THE
PRESIDENTIAL
DEBATE,
1968

THE
PRESIDENTIAL
DEBATE,
1968

STEIN AND DAY/*Publishers*/New York

David Frost Talks With

Vice-President Hubert H. Humphrey

Senator Robert F. Kennedy

Mayor John V. Lindsay

Senator Eugene J. McCarthy

The Hon. Richard M. Nixon

Governor Ronald Reagan

Governor Nelson Rockefeller

The Hon. Harold Stassen

The Hon. George Wallace

Published simultaneously in Canada by Saunders of Toronto Ltd.
Designed by David Miller/Bernard Schleifer
Printed in the United States of America

Stein and Day/Publishers/7 East 48 Street, New York, N.Y. 10017

David Frost and the publishers would like to acknowledge the kind cooperation of Group W, Westinghouse Broadcasting, in the preparation and production of this book.

Contents

Foreword

In any political campaign, one of the many problems confronting the voter is that of attempting to compare the array of candidates placed before him.

The intention of the conversations in this book is to provide such a comparison by recording the differences and similarities as each of the nine leaders responds not only to questions directed solely at him but also to a group of questions posed to most if not all of them.

I am grateful to the candidates for finding the time to relax and talk during the most testing months of their lives in what is now undoubtedly—at least to my eyes—the liveliest democracy in the world; and to those who are, alas, destined to disappointment in America this year, I can only add fervently that there are a great many "situations vacant" in the Leadership business in Europe!

David Frost
Los Angeles, 5 May 1968

The Hon. Richard M. Nixon

DAVID FROST: Mr. Nixon, whenever I travel in America, people always say to me, well, of course, this isn't the real America. The real, typical America is so-and-so. If you had to pick one location as the real, typical ground-base America, where would you pick?

RICHARD NIXON: I think you really can't pick one place. I've often heard people say that Washington, D.C., is not America. No capital of any country is. New York City is not America, it's the financial capital. I find, for example, that a small town in Iowa may be America to me at some time, or out in the far West. The sophistication of San Francisco, or the great vigor of Chicago. My view is that what makes America is its diversity and only if you understand that diversity do you understand America.

FROST: Are there any essentially American characteristics?

NIXON: Of the American people, yes. One characteristic is what I would call a rather hopeless idealism. In view of the criticism around the world today of our activities in Vietnam, I suppose that sounds almost unbelievable, but the American people, at this time in our history when we have such great responsibility in foreign affairs, are idealistic in the tradition of Woodrow Wilson immediately after World War I. Americans really believe their mission in the world, if they have a mission, is not to expand Americanism, so-called, but really to try to work for a world in which everybody can choose. This is one of the reasons that I don't think we're believed abroad because many of the older civilizations just can't understand how it is that Americans can say we're fighting in Vietnam for the right of the Vietnamese to choose their own form of government, or we're fighting in Vietnam so that all nations in the Pacific can have peace. Now incidentally, having raised the Vietnam issue, let me say that many Americans would disagree with what I have just indicated is the American objective, but the American people generally cast their role in the world as an idealistic role and not a pragmatic role.

FROST: In an election year everyone naturally is sort of a doctor diagnosing ills—and suggesting remedies for what ails America. John Lindsay says it's the cities, and Ronald Reagan feels that it's a loosening of morals. What do you think at root is wrong? What is responsible for any malaise there may be?

NIXON: Well, I think it gets down to this. We are today the best fed, best housed, best clothed people in the world or that any civilization in the world has ever achieved, and we find that having achieved that, it isn't enough. This malaise exists primarily among those who are best fed, best housed, best clothed. It exists at a time when the people of the United States for the most part have never had it better. I don't mean by that there aren't terrible areas of poverty, pockets of poverty, in this country, and Americans are concerned about it; but the people of the United States need a dream, they need a vision, they need a purpose bigger than themselves. As a matter of fact, my travels in Europe and other countries lead me to the conclusion that people there need it, too. I found talking to young people in your country, for example, and young people on the continent, the young people in France and Germany and the rest, that they aren't satisfied simply with the achievement of material gains. I think that what the world needs basically at this point is an idealistic goal.

FROST: For an American today, what can that dream or that goal be?

NIXON: Well, it cannot be the dream that might have been possible at the end of the nineteenth century, manifest destiny, the expansion of American domination. It can't be the dream that the British had during their years of colonialism or that the French before them had.

FROST: And the French have got it again.

NIXON: That's right. I think that's the case. But it can be something else, working toward a world in which we can have peace and the right to choose by all peoples abroad; and in the United States, working toward a society which goes beyond what I would call simply the negative freedoms. You remember Franklin Roosevelt's four freedoms?

FROST: Right.

NIXON: Freedom from fear and freedom from want. That was enough in the Thirties because to achieve that goal would have been magnificent. Now, most Americans have achieved it, and they find it isn't enough. Now we must move to what I call Freedoms *to*. Freedoms to travel, freedoms to choose, freedoms to expand one's vision about the world and the purpose of his nation in the world. Leaders must take Americans to the mountain top and show them what that goal is and then see to it that we do meet that goal.

FROST: How could the Americans have a greater freedom to choose than they've got now?

NIXON: Well, they can have a greater freedom to choose in the sense that other people in America and people in the world will also have that freedom. We cannot be satisfied with simply having enough for ourselves. We can only be satisfied when that dream is shared by and is available to all others. Now, I'm not suggesting that there aren't many Americans that don't think completely in selfish terms. Our hippies say we must do our thing. Every person must do his thing. That isn't enough even for them because just doing your thing means that a life can be lived and still be quite empty, because unless in every life an individual at some point in time is engaged in a cause bigger than himself, that life can be a very empty one.

FROST: Do you believe in the principle, "My country, right or wrong?"

NIXON: No, I don't believe in that principle, and I don't believe that many Americans today believe in that principle. I believe incidentally that America in its foreign policy is more right than wrong, but I believe that every American has the responsibility to look at his country's policies and when they are wrong, to do everything he can to right them. I, however, do not believe in what is really the old jingoistic line that whatever America is engaged in we do not criticize it.

FROST: How much is the world changing? How would you define, for instance, today, the word "Communist"? I mean, it's changed. It's no longer a monolithic international conspiracy, would you say?

NIXON: You put your finger on a conclusion that most Americans—most people in the world—need to understand better. I'm somewhat of an expert in this field. At least I've lived with the problem for over twenty years. Twenty years ago, it could be said that Communism was monolithic, with its power center in the Soviet Union. Today, that great Communist monolith is split in half, the Chinese half and the Soviet half. When we look at the Soviet half, or the European half, it is splintering in eight or nine different directions. While there is a mainstream that runs through all Communist philosophy, the Marxist economic principles, nevertheless, within the Communist empire, if it can be called an empire, we find many diverse doctrines fighting for power. Consequently, Communism today, while it is not fragmented nearly to the extent that the non-Communist world is because of the lack of the right of people to choose, nevertheless leaders within the Communist world are beginning to develop the nationalistic tendencies that will inevitably fragment it.

FROST: Would you say then there's any difference basically between a Fascist dictatorship and a Communist dictatorship now?

NIXON: Their means are the same. Their ends are different. To oversimplify a very complicated subject, the Communist goal is one that perhaps many people would not disagree with because they look for a world, not just a nation, but a world in which everyone will receive according to his needs and everyone will contribute according to his ability. Now, that goal is not achievable, as they found in the Soviet Union. They had to turn away from the Marxist theories and have gone to an incentive system in order to get production from their people. Now, the Fascists, on the other hand, tend to be more nationalistic in terms of their goal. Fascism can succeed and can exist in a country without any intention to spread beyond. Now, of course, many will say, well, what about Hitler? He became an aggressive exponent of Fascism and tried to extend it over the balance of Europe, but basically, even Hitler's

13

Fascism was nationalistic in character. Communism is basically international in its thrust, whereas Fascism is more turned inward toward nationalism.

FROST: And in the light of these new definitions, how would you define an un-American activity today?

NIXON: An un-American activity would be any activity which runs counter to the American ideal in the broadest sense of freedom of choice, which we believe we stand for in this country and which is what we really want for the rest of the world. Let me make one thing very clear. There are some Americans who believe our system is so good everybody else ought to have it. I don't share that view. I believe that there are many civilizations that frankly would not have the kind of progress they should have under our system. Some of the underdeveloped countries could not have the kind of progress that they need if they were to apply the American free enterprise system. They simply are not ready for it. I believe that each nation in various periods of development must have the kind of system which best fits that nation and which its people may want. Now, as far as an un-American activity is concerned, it could be in the broadest sense described as one that denies to individuals the right to choose and one that repudiates that doctrine.

FROST: I agree with you. It's very difficult and dangerous to transplant our own conceptions. It was the same with our Westminster system of democracy going to Africa. You know, we say now that the British constitution is the model for constitutions which half the independent nations of Africa have overthrown.

NIXON: Could I interrupt you there? I'm not one of those who believes that colonialism was an unmixed evil. Let's take British colonialism for one moment—and I don't say this because you happen to be British—but British co-

14

lonialism left a great legacy for good in Asia and Africa and in the United States in the Americas. Look at the institutions that are universal. I refer to the common law. I refer to the parliamentary system. I refer to the right of dissent. All of this came from the great British heritage. Now, as far as the British economic system of the nineteenth century was concerned, or the British economic system of the middle of the twentieth century, (which is more, shall we say, socialism), it is that system that I say could not and should not be expanded and might not work in other parts of the world. But when we talk about the right of an individual to have a trial and the right to have freedom of expression—these institutions I think are universal.

FROST: Looking at your career, Mr. Nixon, what would you say is the one achievement that you're most proud of thus far?

NIXON: Well, it wouldn't be the fact that I was elected to the Congress or to the Senate or as Vice-President of the United States, and it wouldn't be the fact that I was selected as the nominee of my party in 1960. All of these were great achievements and at the beginning of my career, I would say that any one of those would have been enough. It isn't what I became, but what I did as Vice-President, particularly in the international field, traveling to most of the countries of the world and possibly making some contribution to a kind of a world in which we can have peace in the last third of this century. Now, at the present time, with the war going on in Vietnam, it seems that that achievement is far away, but I am utterly convinced that the leaders of the United States and of other nations who share our views in the world have as their primary goal— they must have in this last third of the century—the development of policies which will avoid such wars as we had in the second third of the century. I think we made some progress in that direction during the Eisenhower Administration and if we get another chance, I think we can make some more progress during the next administration.

FROST: Is there any episode you'd like to rewrite?

NIXON: Oh, I suppose the answer which first comes to mind is the campaign of 1960. Should I or should I not have debated with John Kennedy on television? And if I did debate him, then perhaps I should have had, as some people have said, a better makeup man and the rest. I think all of that, however, is rather beside the point. I would not try to Monday morning quarterback the things that I did as Vice-President or as a campaigner. Mistakes were made. I prefer to look to the future, and as far as those mistakes are made, I'll try not to make as many.

FROST: Right, I just wondered if there was one remark, for instance, you—looking back—wish you hadn't said, or something like that. I think we've all got those, probably.

NIXON: Many people will say that the statement that I should not have made was my criticism of the press when I lost for Governor of California, and I would answer that question now in this way. As a public man looking forward to the possibility of again running for office, to have made that statement was a very great mistake. When I first entered politics, a very wise old politician gave me some very good advice. He said, now Dick, I want to tell you something. You're going to make many mistakes during the course of your political career, but remember this: never get into an argument with the press because they always have the last word. However, when I finished that campaign for Governor of California, I didn't have any idea that I would ever be sitting where I am today, being interviewed as a potential candidate for the Presidency of the United States. A private citizen has a right to express his views when he thinks he's being put upon. However, as a public figure, I would say that that was a mistake, and I can also assure you that as far as getting in an argument with the press, it won't happen again as long as I'm a public figure.

FROST: But once you're not, you can have a go! Do you in fact recognize the picture of yourself you see in the press? Is there one thing about you that you feel doesn't get enough play in the press?

NIXON: Well now, I'm not going to get in the business of criticizing the press again!

FROST: Say one thing you'd add to the—

NIXON: —to the picture of the press?

FROST: Yes.

NIXON: I suppose every political man feels that his critics in the press and otherwise make a mistake when they question the sincerity of his views. Now, every political man has to be somewhat pragmatic. I look at our potential opponents on the other side. I know them all well. I presided over the Senate when two of them were in the Senate and I knew Bobby Kennedy in other ways. I couldn't disagree more with them on some issues, but I believe that each of those men is a patriotic American. I believe each of them is for peace, and I believe questioning his motives is below the belt. I believe in fighting hard. I'll fight hard on the issues. Now, if I were to ask for any treatment from the press or my critics, it would be that I don't mind their questioning my tactics, how I express myself, my appearance on television. I can't do anything about my face. I've tried and there it is, and no make-up man can cure it. All this I don't mind, but when they go to the point of saying well, this man really isn't for peace because he stands for a firm line in Vietnam or in the mid-East or someplace else, then I say that's the kind of criticism that I think could well be left alone. Let me just add one other point. I'm greatly concerned about this election in America, not because I'm in it. I'm concerned for that reason, of course, but I'm also concerned because of what it could do to the soul of America. All elections are hard fought in this country, and elections in wartime are particularly difficult. What we find now is that when the various people who disagree on Vietnam go on our college campuses and are shouted down that an ugly streak shows in the American people, a streak which really is, I think, rather foreign to our point of view. Now, I know that in Britain you can have some very vigorous debate, and I've appeared at Oxford and know how those questions bang back and forth. That's altogether different. At least usually a man is given the right there and has been given the right here to express his views and is respected for a different point of view, and I would just hope that in this campaign that some of the shrillness and some of the meanness could go out of the debate. Let's hit hard, but let's get away from these personal charges. For example in the New Hampshire campaign, where President Johnson was running against Eugene McCarthy, some of the people carried a disgraceful sign, "Hey, Hey, LBJ. How Many Kids Did You Kill Today?" Then on the other side, of course, there was a reaction from the Johnson forces, and they attacked Senator McCarthy, who is a very sincere man. I think I have to disagree with what he says about Vietnam, but not to attack him in saying that Senator McCarthy, by raising the question of our commitment in Vietnam, was deliberately giving aid and comfort to Ho Chi Minh. Senator McCarthy is for peace, and so is Lyndon Johnson. I know Lyndon Johnson doesn't want to have any American boys killed, just as Senator McCarthy doesn't want to have them killed, but the larger question is not just ending the war in Vietnam. It's winning the peace. It's easy to end a war. The question is, do you win the peace for the next generation. I think we should debate that hard, but let's get away from questioning motives. Now, they can say what they want about me. I've been heckled by experts, so it doesn't make any difference what they say about me.

FROST: Just for a moment, taking a wider question, as you look back at history, which historical character would you say you most admire, or you feel most in sympathy with?

NIXON: Well, I suppose like most Americans, it would be Abraham Lincoln. In terms of our American political figures—I will leave out the historical characters of the other countries because there are many there that I admire too—but the American political figures—Abraham Lincoln, Theodore Roosevelt, and Woodrow Wilson, leaving out the ones in the latest generation, of course, I think those three Presidents—two of them were Republicans, one was a Democrat—some way captured the American dream of what I call this hopeless idealism, combined with the vigorous drive which is characteristic of America.

FROST: This is a vast question, I know, but at root, what would you say that people are on earth for?

NIXON: If I had to answer that question in the middle of our depression, when I was attending law school, it would have been that people are on earth for the purpose of just existing. In other words, freedom from fear and freedom from want, being well clothed, well fed, well housed. But now that we have reached that floor, that goal, at least for most people in America and for most people in western Europe and in Britain, we have to look beyond that; I believe that people are on earth for a greater vision, a greater purpose, and that is to share with others the dreams that they already have achieved. In their way, those who have accepted the Communist ideology have that point of view. That's what's given them their drive. It isn't just empire that drives the Communist on. It's their belief that the way of life that they stand for will make a better world, a peaceful world, and also one in which there may be more plenty, but I think they're wrong in so far as their philosophy is concerned.

Abraham Lincoln put it best when he said that "our goal is to give everybody an equal chance at the starting line." He did not say that our goal should be to give people the housing and the jobs and everything that they want, but an equal chance at the starting line. If my children and their grandchildren can grow up in a world in which all people have an equal chance at the starting line and to develop to the full their creative abilities, then we are going to have progress just undreamed of. We're going to break into the unknown, and it will be an exciting and interesting world. We must drive forward and upward and onward. We must have the lift of a driving dream. Now, I haven't answered your question, and the reason is that when anybody gives you a precise answer to that question, he misses the American dream.

FROST: You mentioned earlier that in 1962 you thought you were going to leave public life and return to personal life and you didn't. What was the final thing that decided you?

NIXON: Well, at that point of time, I was going to leave public life not as a matter of choice, but because the public wanted me to leave. I'm a believer in the proposition that the individual cannot really go out and say, "Look, here I am, people. I'm going to be your Governor, or your

Senator, or your Congressman, or your President," unless people want him to do it; and in 1962, after that defeat in California, I was convinced that I was not the man for the times at that point and I was willing to accept that decision. Then events changed that. As a result of the Republican division in '54 and as a result, too, of the great foreign policy crises, what I stood for seemed to be what the country needed. Now, when I say "country," that sounds like a self-serving statement, and maybe it's intended to be, but what I really mean is that a great number of people in the country felt that I had a point of view and a type of experience that the nation might need for leadership at this point. And if those events hadn't occurred, I wouldn't be here today. Nothing that I could have done would have changed it.

FROST: I think a great many people sort of marveled at and admired your comeback, your fightback. Do you, in a purely human sort of personal sense, do you sometimes look back to '62 and pinch yourself to see if '68 is true?

NIXON: I know that your people in Britain like to take a little wager, and I would say that in 1962, when I finished that campaign for Governor of California, I would have taken a bet of a million to one that I would never be running for public office again, although I'd always have an interest in public affairs; and as I look back on these last seven and a half years, I marvel at what's happened. I don't mean by that that we are just little chips on the great stream of fate and that there's nothing we can do to change it. A man must be ready. He must be prepared. He must be willing. He can't just sit back and wait for that draft to occur and I'm that kind of an activist. But unless the events are ready for the man at the time—

both must come together—the man must be ready and the country and the events and the time must be ready. When they come together, then you have that chemical reaction which means success.

FROST: How would you define political success?

NIXON: When I first entered politics, I would have defined political success just as winning. When I ran for Congress the first time—winning for Congress at thirty-two years of age—that was an immense achievement to me and to my wife, our family; but now, having had virtually everything that a man can have in terms of being somebody—I've been a Congressman, a Senator, and a Vice-President, and almost a President—success now would mean only being able to do something. Unless in the process of running for President I can contribute to the debate which will create a better chance for peace abroad and for peace and progress at home, my life will have been a failure.

FROST: And how would you like to be remembered? It's a long way ahead, but what would you like the first line of your obituary in the *New York Times* to say?

NIXON: "He made a great contribution to the peace of the world." This probably goes back to a family situation. My mother and my grandmother were very devout birthright Quakers and I became, as a participant in World War II and as an antagonist and a very vigorous one in political campaigns, very un-Quakerish in their eyes. But deep down, there runs through me, as there does I think in most Americans, a deep desire for a better world in which we can really have peace. If I don't make a contribution to it, my life will have been a failure.

FROST: You were talking earlier on about everyone having an equal chance at the starting line. How soon do you think the Negro in America will have an equal chance at the starting line?

NIXON: Legally, we have achieved that goal. That wasn't the case a hundred years ago when the Negro had the Emancipation Proclamation. It could be said then that Lincoln freed the slaves, and now our task is to free the Negro. We've done that from the standpoint of legislation over the past ten years—the historic bills that have been passed by the Congress of the United States—but that's only the beginning. What we now have to do after opening doors is to prepare the Negro to walk through those doors. What we now have to do after a period of revolution is to have a period of reconciliation. Let me explain. For the Negro to have an equal chance, it just mustn't be in terms of, well, he has the right to buy a house, he has a right to a job. But he must have somebody on the other side of the table who is willing not only to obey the law legally to its letter, but to carry it out in spirit, and that means a new spirit among the white people in this country, of reconciliation between the two great races, rather than this wall of hatred that has been built up in this period of revolution.

FROST: In other words, you're saying there has been a history of what the riot report said was white racism, and that's—

NIXON: I would question it in this respect. There has been white racism, and there has been black racism in this country, and there will continue to be. I would also say, however, that white racism is not characteristic of the great body of the American people. What we have overlooked and what the Commission overlooked is that the whole period of this revolution legally wouldn't have been possible unless a majority of the white people in this country recognized that racism was wrong and wanted to do something about it. Now, what we have to do is quit this talking about white racism and black racism and get the races reconciled so that we can really move forward.

FROST: George Wallace really is going to be a racist candidate in a sense. Do you think he'll get many votes?

NIXON: I suppose that he would deny that he would be a racist candidate.

FROST: He would be seen as such.

NIXON: He will be getting a pretty big vote from some of those who may think in those terms. My guess is, though, that the Wallace vote will get progressively lower as the contest between the two top contenders gets hotter because what happens in our country is the third party candidates get very small votes in any close elections. Nineteen forty-eight is a case in point, where Henry Wallace, who took a very different point of view from his namesake—Henry Wallace got only a million votes. He was predicted to get five million, and I think that George Wallace—I think he'll get a good vote, but not a decisive vote. I don't think he'll be the kingmaker in this election.

FROST: And so you don't think there's any way really in which black and white are basically different, or do you?

NIXON: Oh, that's the whole point. They are basically different. It makes no contribution to progress in this area to say that white people and black people are the same, that they are equal in every respect. In some respects, I can assure you when I look at some of the athletic contests and other areas where our Negro citizens have had an equal chance, they can be very superior to some of the white people who compete with them, and in other areas, the whites may be superior. Let's understand this. I get back to our original point. The greatness of America is that we have diversity, that we are not the same. There are

24

black people and white people. There are people with Italian backgrounds and Irish backgrounds and the rest, and the fact that we are different gives diversity to life and I wouldn't want to change that. I don't want Americans to be just one, great conglomerate mass with no distinction among them. I think having this competition, the friendly competition among people, is a good thing, but let's be sure that the competition is fair; and that means giving every-body an equal chance at the line and then giving those who haven't had their chance, who've had it denied for a hundred years, that little extra start that they need so that it is in truth an equal chance. That's our goal.

Senator Eugene J. McCarthy

DAVID FROST: Senator, what would you say is your ideal America? What would be your ideal America?

SENATOR EUGENE J. MCCARTHY: It's a rather hard opening question. I think we were beginning to move toward something that was approaching the ideal in the years from '62 and '63. We reached a point where it seemed at least we had mastered the problems of the economy to a point where we could begin to meet the economic needs of the people and establish the material base for not a limited education program, but one which was reaching out so as to make the most talented as well as the least gifted of our country within the range of educational opportunity. We had begun to move, I think, to develop a kind of restrained attitude toward the rest of the world, not attempting really to impose a rather ill-defined concept of what America stood for on Africa, for example, where we were quite open; and it appears as though we were willing to take a chance or two on revolution in Latin America. We weren't coming quite so quickly to understand the differences between Europe and America and to understand that those differences would probably last for a long time, but I think there was an adjustment taking place. It is as though we ac-

26

cepted we were part of the movement of history instead of the nineteenth-century-early-twentieth-century attitude that somehow we stood apart from it. We could step in and out, or we could give it a push in this direction or in that; and this kind of self-knowledge, I think, of America in the sense of its limited purpose, but of almost unlimited potential, I think was the kind of America we've been talking about. Some people have been talking about it for a hundred years, but we'd never really come close to the realization of it.

FROST: What is the essence of being American really? I mean, what are the characteristics that distinguish the American, would you say?

MCCARTHY: Well, generally, we've left that kind of analysis to the British, you know. It's been their strength to come over—

FROST: We just gaze at our own navels, now.

MCCARTHY: Yes, now you've turned in upon yourselves in your insecurity, but until recently, we were really concerned only about criticism the British might direct at us; and now that you've turned it upon yourselves, we'll have to begin to examine our own characters somewhat more intimately, I suppose! No, I think we had a kind of conception of America as a kind of the land of the innocent and the preordained; this was a concept from which we had to escape, and I think we were escaping from it. I could use, you know, the generalization that we reached the point of maturity. I think this is what Adlai Stevenson had begun to talk about when he was candidate for the Presidency and when he spoke about America, and we were moving on from that. An idea that it wasn't just two or three great heroic virtues that characterized us as we had more or less believed in the last century, but that it was a conception of the country as having a somewhat broader base in virtues, not all of which were heroic—some of which will be traditionally classified as somewhat unheroic.

FROST: If you had to pick one place that is real, typical America, where would that be?

McCARTHY: Oh, I think it's probably whichever place you're in somehow.

FROST: Particularly if you're campaigning.

McCARTHY: That's right. You know, I don't think New Hampshire, for example, which was my first primary state was untypical certainly. There were elements of it which were different from my own state, but the core of it was pretty much the same, the same interests, the same concern, the same distractions. Even the South, I think, which twenty years ago, at least in the period before World War II, was somewhat isolated, has come on to be more and more a part of and more and more like the rest of the country and the West, so that the old regionalism which once had some substance in this country no longer really has much meaning.

FROST: And who would you say now represents what is to you the best of the United States?

McCARTHY: If I were referring to a group that I think have come close to representing what I think the real America is, I think it would probably be the students and the young people of the country who have, for whatever the reasons may be, good or bad, broken out of the old mold and are approaching the problem with a new kind of freedom of intellect and without the sense of guilt or the limitations of the old prejudices or the false conceptions which marked America.

FROST: Someone like Governor Reagan, on the other hand, would probably point at them with horror of their long hair and everything as the sign that the country was going to the dogs.

McCARTHY: Yes, I think that he must have some worries about them, but I think that broadly based, this is the best representation. I don't mean to say that it's only among the young people because I think the adults are concerned. They may not be very responsive to them, but they are concerned more than ever before in the history of the country—at least in the time that I've looked at it, in politics especially—more concerned, more disturbed over what the young people may think or what the difference is between what they think and what the young people of America are willing to accept, whether it's race relations at home or whether it's something like the Peace Corps service overseas which took on almost a religious character, which was kind of a shock to some Americans who never thought of that kind of dedicated service as being a direct function of a government program; you may say well, we have a Presbyterian mission, or a Methodist mission, or a Catholic mission. That was understandable, but to have it in a way of a kind of nondenominational, public-spirited manifestation, some people were surprised.

FROST: We were talking earlier on about when you started out on this campaign and so on and getting known and all that sort of thing. Now, if you were talking on the phone to someone who was meeting you who didn't happen to know what you looked like, how would you describe yourself?

McCARTHY: As to what I look like, or what I am?

FROST: As to how they should recognize you.

McCARTHY: Oh, I haven't really thought much about that. I wouldn't really go much for comparisons. I've had some terrible descriptions of me, you know, by some of the columnists along the way about being a gray spirit in a gray body and a gray voice, and I don't think that's quite right.

29

FROST: That's an interesting thing. Do you recognize generally the picture of yourself in the press, or do you sometimes feel it's somewhat of a different person?

McCARTHY: Well, some of them I think have read me pretty well, but they run in fads here, especially the columnists. I'm not sure that the column is a really good device. It calls for a kind of short-range, rash judgment, especially when they write three columns a week. Three rash judgments a week are really too much to expect of anybody. So if one does it, the other is hard-pressed and likely to pick up the same theme; so they go around in circles. Then they'll change the line, and we say it's like blackbirds on the telephone line here in the fall. If one flies away they all fly away. If one comes back, they all come back down. I've been moved to be somewhat more sympathetic to the conservative columnists in the course of my campaign than the more liberal ones whom I expected to be somewhat friendly to my cause but who began analyzing me pretty much in terms of some kind of psychological disturbance to explain why we're doing this. Whereas the conservatives have explained it in terms of rather simple primitive vices like anger and jealousy or envy, words which have been lost to the vocabulary until recently, and I think I'd prefer to be accused of being envious or angry than neurotic or frustrated, or whatever it might be. I think we'll work it out all right as we go along!

FROST: Who is the historical character you most admire?

McCARTHY: It would probably have to be a composite of some kind. I've kind of got me hitched to Thomas More. A *New York Times* writer read *Utopia* and decided that had to be it, you know. I've kind of given up denying—you get to a point where you just don't deny, you accept. I think he was a rather interesting man because he was kind of a breakthrough. He had to accept responsibility more or less outside the pattern of a tradition or of family obligation. I rather admire Edmund Burke for what he said. I don't think he was the best politician around, but he had good ideas. I think, of the modern politicians, Harry Truman was probably the best President we had, really, in that he had a clear conception of what the office was and what could be done within the office which is what we need in this country. There's a tendency to overpersonalize the Presidency here, to take it on as though you know you had captured it somehow. It's kind of the Yorks and the Lancasters, you know. It's ours now. We'll run it, not just personalize the style, which the Kennedys did. That's quite all right, but there is a tendency also to personalize the manner in which the office is conducted, and I thought Truman always pretty well kept the lines clear as to what was his responsibility as the President and what was the Congressional responsibility, what the role of the military was in the case of General MacArthur—and to say: all right, if you want to be a general, be a general. If you want to be a politician, why, you know, you can resign, or we'll ask you to resign. You can come back and run for President if you want to, but we're not going to let you run the two together, and so on through most of the tests that occurred in the Truman Administration. The lines were pretty well drawn, and I think it is important, at least for the long pull, that we do kind of clarify the institutional lines of government. I feel they're being eroded.

FROST: In all your political career, what would you say is the most important or memorable phrase that you've created or coined?

MCCARTHY: Oh, I don't know. I suppose it's the speech that I gave for Stevenson, the one in which I said, "Do not reject this man." That's not altogether original I

31

suppose! It's been said before. Most everything one says has been said before. At least it was original as far as I was concerned at the time, and it seemed to have marked at least that particular speech in the minds of the people.

FROST: Is there any one episode that as you look back —at the moment you're mainly looking forward—but thus far, is there any one single episode in your life that you'd like to rewrite?

McCARTHY: I suppose there are a few personal ones. I don't think there are any political ones. I've had rather good fortune in politics. It moved along pretty well. No disappointments. I think I've kept the lines of integrity, as far as I could, pretty well clear—it hasn't got tangled up too much.

FROST: You're a religious man. Are there specific issues you can point to where your religious beliefs have affected your political stance?

McCARTHY: In a limited sense of religious positions, I wouldn't say so. I think there have been four or five issues we've had in which the moral component has been quite high, and I don't know whether out of religion I was stronger for it than I otherwise would have been. Things like the early effort to do something about migratory farm labor in this country which involved great injustice. The whole civil rights fight, the test ban treaty, and I think, you know, as I went along by way of changing position or passing judgment on the war, as the war itself changed. The disposition to pass a moral judgment on an issue of this kind did have some bearing upon the action I've taken. I thought it reached a point where it was not morally justified, not just a question of being in the national interest —I think one can oppose the war on that basis alone—but it was not morally justified.

FROST: If you had to choose one adjective to describe

President Johnson's Administration, what would be the first one that comes to mind?

McCARTHY: Well, I was asked that some time ago. I replied by asking whether the person had ever read a good critical review of an accordion concert—it was simply a matter of how do you break through! This was before the war became the issue, but I think it's still much the same thing. It's a question of going back to what I said about the confusion of the kind of homogenization which has taken place, so it's awfully hard to find a point of breakthrough even on the war. When did it start? Who made the decisions? It's the idea of escalation, or homogenization, and of the general confusion of lines.

FROST: But if you had to find one word above all else to describe the Johnson Administration—

McCARTHY: I think I would say it has been personalized in keeping with the character of the President. Then you have to go on saying—well, what do you mean? What's the personality of the President? But I think this is a particular mark of it. Much more so than was true of the Kennedy Administration where you knew pretty well the lines of thought on economics, for example, and on foreign policy. These were set more or less by the position of the party and also by the kind of people whom you knew would be consulted. This has not been true with reference to President Johnson. It's personalized and highly variable.

FROST: This is a long way ahead, but how would you like to be remembered? How would you like the first line of your obituary to read?

McCARTHY: "He died," I suppose. That would be most reassuring.

FROST: That's granted. Now the second sentence.

McCARTHY: Well, I've been saying that really if you become President of the United States, you ought to be indifferent to what your biographers might say about you or the historians. I think this was true about Harry Truman. It made him a great President really. He just said, you know, Harry Truman, President. I think you could extend it. i felt this is what made John XXIII probably the greatest Pope because he was utterly indifferent to what the historians might say about him. I don't think I've reached quite that level of purity myself, but I think one really ought to be somewhat indifferent to what it might really say. I said about Lyndon Johnson in 1960 when I was supporting him before Stevenson became a candidate that I had reservations about him. I thought he might make a good Prime Minister in that he would then be subject to the discipline of the party and of the minister and also, of course, the potential of bringing down the government if you had to, but that I had reservations about him in the office of the Presidency to really move the country if a new challenge arose of some kind.

FROST: Would you like our Prime Minister then?

McCARTHY: Well, I don't know whether I want your Prime Minister. I was thinking about the system. The Foreign Relations Committee, the whole committee by better than two to one is opposed to our foreign policy. If we had a cabinet system, a Prime Minister would be subject to that restraint and to that discipline. We would have a different foreign policy.

FROST: Do you believe in the principle, "My country, right or wrong"?

McCARTHY: No. Of course, that isn't really quite the principle here. There are some qualifying phrases after that to the end that if it was right, why, you did everything that ought to be done and if it was wrong, you tried to change the policy. Now I don't accept this phrase although this is a kind of slogan that the former Cardinal Archbishop of

New York quoted, not completely, but within the limits which the clergy sometimes reserve to themselves.

FROST: Does the word Communism mean the same thing now that it did in a world-wide sense ten years ago?

McCARTHY: I suppose that it doesn't. I feel it's one of those words that changes meaning as history moves, and even Dean Rusk is beginning to use qualifying adjectives. He speaks of Asian Communism now which he didn't used to speak about fifteen years ago, he spoke of the Communism in China as simply an extension of Russian Communism. He described it as a kind of Slavic Manchukuo dynasty but he now has a new kind of Communism, which he calls Asian.

FROST: Is there any difference, would you say, between a Communist dictatorship and a Fascist dictatorship?

McCARTHY: Well, I think there is a difference in the totality of the Communist dictatorships as they've emerged historically as distinguished from the Fascist ones and the manner in which they've developed—I think there is a somewhat different response on the part of the people in support of the dictatorship, even though they may be dominated. I mean, there's always a playback of support from some of the people in the society. I think the Nazi dictatorship had a different kind of support and a different kind of interplay between the dictator and the people than you have, for example, in a Russian dictatorship.

FROST: How would you therefore define patriotism?

McCARTHY: Well, I think there's more patriotism in something like the Russian dictatorship than there was in the German. I think that it was less related to an idea of truly a national state and a national function, and it was a kind of device which more or less personalized fears or desires, whatever they might be. But in this country I think

35

that the old kind of idea that there was something very clear, you know, when you talk about a Communist—that this was what it was and this was a conspiracy and so on, I think that this is no longer generally held.

FROST: This is a very, very big question indeed, but—

McCARTHY: Some of them you've asked me up to now have been reasonably large.

FROST: Well, let's go just slightly bigger then. Basically, at root, what would you say that people are on earth for?

McCARTHY: I could give you the formula, or I can say de Chardin has got the conception—he probably comes as close to telling you what man is here for, where he's going. I don't know whether we're quite sure about why, but I think you have to come to a judgment as to why you're here and let the other people take care of themselves, and it works down, I think, to a conception of some kind of service to the rest of humanity and, at the same time, a kind of perfection of yourself in terms of what you think and how much you can grasp and what can be known and what you can do by way, I suppose, of some appreciation of what the beautiful is and how you can bring it to others. It's a triple sort of thing, I suppose, the idea of coming to know as much as you can and of reflecting it somehow and also of transmitting it so far as you can to other people. This, of course, involves religion and philosophy and the whole structure of society, but I think you have to kind of back it up to yourself to the point almost where you're not sure of whether there are really any other people on earth, one or two maybe.

FROST: Not to waste one's time or talents in effect.

McCARTHY: That's it really. It doesn't mean that you can't be somewhat selfish, I suppose, and kind of turn in upon yourself. I mean, I don't have the idea of full public service. I think there is a place for some private life.

FROST: If we were looking now at the political map of the world in ten year's time, in what main ways would it be different from today, do you think?

McCARTHY: Oh, I don't think it would be very different from what it is now. I think you might have more stability in Africa. I think there would be some significant improvements in Latin America. I'm hopeful that a country like Brazil will come along all right. As far as Asia is concerned, I think that there would be little change there unless we persist in making it. We're either in or out of Vietnam. I don't think it will make a significant difference in southeastern Asia. I anticipate that the European countries will maintain their independence. The fact that they know they can have some kind of economic interdependence without destroying their culture I think probably argues against the kind of political consolidation that people thought was necessary after the end of World War II. Also in view of the new weapons and the decreased likeliness of war, the tendency to retain a kind of personal identification on the part of the nations of Europe, I think is likely to be strengthened rather than weakened. If we could just work out something by which we could save England, why we'd be all right.

FROST: The size of the British Empire might just continue to decline a little?

McCARTHY: Well, it might a little bit, but I think as long as the United States is as dependent on the pound as it is now, we'll have to save you somehow!

FROST: Thank you very much.

Governor Ronald Reagan

DAVID FROST: Wherever I go in America, people say, this isn't the real America. The real America is so-and-so. What geographical spot would you point to, do you think, to explain America?

GOVERNOR RONALD REAGAN: Well, I don't know whether I'd choose a geographical spot, but I think I'd choose a smaller town. Now, you may say, but with most of the people living in the city, how would this be typical of America? Well, most of the people living in the city came from those small towns; and whether they're willing to admit it or not, there is something from that small town upbringing that stays with most Americans, even in the city. And somehow the pace—there is a sense of value that —well, as far back as you want to go into history, this has been recognized. Jefferson, in explaining why our system seemed to be a little overbalanced in favor of the countrymen against the city folk, remarked—even back that far in our young country—as he called them, the yeomanry did have a more solid set of values and a better approach to things than people who were crowded into the highly competitive atmosphere of the city.

FROST: Are there any characteristics that are really American?

REAGAN: Oh yes, and I think the world has seen an

38

example of it. Now don't get me wrong, I don't want to sound chauvinistic or like the usual American tourist boasting about his country, but I think there is a generosity that is inherent in American people. I think of the great worldwide program of aid. Many countries and even some of your countrymen have remarked that they wonder what other nation would have embarked on such a thing. I think there's also still a kind of pioneer heritage of the American —well, the military talked about it, the professional soldiers, not only of our own country, but of other countries in wars. They talked about how this citizen army that would be mustered such as for World War I and II had kind of, well, cut through the red tape and never mind the book. Tell us where we're supposed to be and we'll get there. This, I think, is an American characteristic. There's a third one, and this is probably the least understood in foreign countries when Americans are tourists. We get a reputation for being brash, and we get a reputation for overstepping the bounds of propriety and so forth. We don't wait for someone to contact us. I think Americans are kind of like puppy dogs. They love everybody, and they can't see why everybody doesn't love them, so when they go visiting some other country, they want to walk up, knock on the door, and stick out their hand and say, Hello, I'm Joe Smith from Arkansas.

FROST: I think that's very true. I've experienced the friendliness a great deal, I must say. You mentioned a solid set of values just now, talking about small town America. In an election year, everybody is sort of analyzing the country. One reads in all the journals about a malaise in America. What is it that really worries you?

REAGAN: Well, is it just American, or isn't it worldwide?

FROST: It may very well be.

REAGAN: You read of campus riots, and you think that

you're reading about your own state, and you suddenly look back up at the dateline and realize that it's in some foreign capital that it's happened. There seems to be a great rise now of nationalism, for example. Instead of the tendency we thought would follow World War II by way of the United Nations, of the world forgetting boundaries and coming together, it's the other way around now. We started out in this country a few years ago in our minority communities with a drive toward more equal opportunities, and this ambition was shared by all of us; even the majority, the bulk of the people, wanted equal opportunity for all, but suddenly it's taken a turning and you find that some of our minority groups are not talking integration or equal opportunity any more. They're talking separation. They're talking about setting up their own community. Now, I think part of this, we have to recognize, is helped along; it's helped along by a force in the world that has followed the Hitlerian technique, if it didn't precede it, the Communist movement, which says one of the ways to further their goals is to find wherever there is a difference between people and widen that difference, get in and foment and disturb. This is just adding to it. They didn't cause it—they're taking advantage of it. I think sometimes in our own country, some of the rebellion on the part of youth is because we, their parents, they have seen us displaying a kind of hypocrisy. We are not ourselves following enough the principles and standards that we try to teach them, so it isn't that they're rebelling against our standards, they're really crying out for someone to give them some standards. I believe that some of the disturbances on the campus are not the result of too much discipline. I think that they're like the small child stomping his feet and what he really wants is a parent to take him in hand and shake him and let him know where the guidelines are, and I think that our younger generation today would like to have someone, namely the older generation, set some guidelines and some rules and say, here, this is the framework. This is the pattern. You stay within that pattern. In this way, we can also give them a banner to follow, a cause to believe in, and I think people are looking for such a cause.

FROST: You talk about a sort of lessening of standards, a loosening of morals. What exactly does that phrase mean? For instance, we think of California as having a tremendously high divorce rate. Is that an indication?

REAGAN: No, we have a highly publicized divorce rate because of the great publicity attendant upon the motion picture colony; and I, as the President of the Screen Actors' Guild, or actors' union, for many years, I used to do some talking publicly about the actual figures and statistics, and what we had in Hollywood that was highly publicized was a small group of people that I call the multiple marriage people. This small group, whatever their personal tragedies were, just didn't seem able to find happiness, and they set the whole tone, when in truth the divorce rate of the Hollywood motion picture colony was a little lower than the national average; so the rest of the people were pretty solid. No, I think California has higher principles or standards as anyone else. I think the decline of morality— well, let me explain—I have a man, a professor, on my staff here as liaison with our higher education institutions; and he told me of an example in his own campus experience of a young girl, one of the coeds, and he was talking to her and she was deeply disturbed about things of this kind and about her own family. She loved them dearly, but her love stopped short of respect; and she told of an incident in which the girls had decided to have a slumber party and had chosen her home. She was to tell her mother that the girls had decided that chaperons were out this season. They'd have that slumber party without—mother and father were going to have to find someplace else to stay during the slumber party, and the girl confessed to him that she was praying that her mother would stop her and would say, "Not on your life. We'll be here chaperoning." She said her mother got on the phone and starting calling other mothers, taking a public opinion poll of what she should do. The girl as I say admitted she didn't believe this chaperonless party was proper, and she wanted someone to give her a rule, to give her a guideline, so she could go back to the girls and even if she complained, be able to say, I can't do it, instead of, I don't want to do it.

FROST: This is really allied to what we've just been saying about rebellion and lawlessness. When you talk about the rising problem of crime in the cities, of violence in the streets, how many different categories does that cover because there are so many things that go on in the streets. I mean, there's the mugger on the one hand, but there's the demonstrations and so on. To what are you really referring?

REAGAN: Well, it covers and is encompassed in this whole thing about the morality gap in our land. It has to do with the increase in crime, of course, and particularly an increase in crimes of violence; but the signs are that it's more than just having more psychotics, more criminals and so forth and the fact is that there is a vast increase in the assaults on symbols of law and order, policemen; the citizen who is not an outright criminal, the groups who will suddenly gather and interfere with a policeman and then be violent and attack him when he's going about his business, perhaps attacking or arresting someone who has broken the law, and they'll—citizens that you know aren't criminals will do this. There's the tendency to demonstrate and picket and break the windows and so forth over some issue

42

prior to the negotiation. Now, once upon a time and I think all of us accepted that in labor disputes, or whatever it might be, there'd come moments in which after long and frustrating negotiations and not getting an answer to their problem, the people might suddenly get mad and throw a rock and say, well, we're going to do something. Today, the demonstration precedes the negotiations. You don't know there's an issue until you suddenly look out the window and here comes the parade with the picket signs and they're ready to push the policemen out of the way. Here in this capital, several weeks ago, a group with the bandoleers of ammunition and the weapons marched into this capitol and into the legislative halls, and it's a little shocking to Americans, even though we have quite a violent history. But it's happening not only here, but around the world. We get transcripts in here all the time of meetings that are being held on various causes from Vietnam to our minority problems, and the things they're advocating— the speakers—not "let us go and present our case to government." They're advocating, "if this happens, we'll kill so-and-so." Revolution is in the air.

FROST: It is a very violent country though, in many ways. I read somewhere you collect guns yourself, don't you?

REAGAN: Well, not from the standpoint of wanting to attack someone, but gun collecting. I'm not a serious collector in the sense of people I know who have fantastic and marvelous collections of guns dating back—historic pieces and so forth. I've always had them. I've lived in the country. I've had a ranch. I'm not a hunter to any extent, shoot varmints now and then to protect the livestock at the ranch, and I like guns. I like target shooting, and I have one or two pieces that aren't actual usable pieces but are collector's items just because I enjoy having them.

FROST: In a country, though, where everyone realizes there may be riots or violence or whatever, guns are incredibly available, aren't they?

REAGAN: Yes, although I'm not one who believes in overdoing the restriction on that because the wrong person can always get the gun, so perhaps it's proper that the right person should have them at least available. I don't believe that the weapon—the gun as a weapon or anything else—is linked to any cause for what is going on or what is disturbing us because—you look at some of our worst mob actions—the use of firearms is fairly recent and fairly new. They seem to be able to revert back to the club and do very well, destructively.

FROST: I was talking to Senator McCarthy, and the questioning students were to him the most optimistic thing about America. I suspect in a sense to you they're the most worrying thing, aren't they?

REAGAN: No, no, let me make one thing plain here. I have repeatedly stated that the real dissident group, the violent group, the demonstrating group, were not questioning. They figure they've got all the answers. They're trying to impose their answers on everyone else. They're a tiny minority. I think that you've got a militant and a violent group on our campuses, very tiny. You've got another group, or two groups—they're divided—but let's put them as one group on two sides that are active politically, that are interested in what's going on politically. They're a great hope, and the bulk of your students are still what they were when we were in school. The bulk of your students are still interested in the things of the campus and what's going on, and they are fairly apathetic about the problems of the world today. They figure they'll tackle those when they get out and become adults. No, the activist group, not the militant group, the activist group that is really concerned and really interested—and we have delegations of them that come here all the time, and I try to figure the schedule any time so that if they're going to be here, we can meet—they impress me. They're bright. They know more than we did. They're more aware of things than we were, and I think they hold out a great promise of hope.

FROST: Do you think sometimes though that there is a possibility that in the situation America is in now some dissent could become so militant that, for instance, some of the traditional methods of democratic debate would have to be curtailed?

REAGAN: Well, of course, that's the pattern of history, to try and curb dissent by oppression or holding it down. I think every country, not just this one, I think every country is faced right now with a great problem of how to handle this. I think that we have to take a firm stand, not on repressing what is normal but simply on enduring, putting up with whatever dissent is within the framework of the law. But I think we have to take a firm stand that the law is supreme and will not be broken, that we have provided in this government—I'm sure other countries certainly have—in England—have provided the citizen with more leeway, more flexibility to change the law, make his wants known, and the law of changes will follow if enough of the people feel that way. We've made all those provisions. They should not be curtailed or changed, but those people who decide which laws they will obey are going to openly break the others; then I say you have to use the full force and authority of the government and of the people to stop that. We must remain nations of laws, or the jungle has come right back to the city limits.

FROST: So your advice to the people who are in favor of the peace in Vietnam would be what?

REAGAN: Why, I think they follow all the normal channels through their elected representatives, impressing their will on them and trying to convince their fellow citizens that they're right. Now, today the Vietnam protesters—I happen to think they're wrong in what they're protesting.

FROST: Wrong period.

REAGAN: But what they're doing that is wrong is they are trying to impose their will and their idea on the people with the very evident fact in front of them that they are not speaking for the majority of the people. Now, if their position was right, their goals should be to persuade. Say the majority of the people want to follow a different course, but here's a little minority that says we don't care what the majority says. We're right and therefore we want the government to obey us, the minority, not the majority.

FROST: So that in fact Senator McCarthy's campaign for instance is the right way to go about it, to try to persuade people.

REAGAN: That's right. Senator McCarthy is doing exactly right, and he can then appeal to all those people who have a chance to stand up and make their wants and their desires known.

FROST: Do you believe in the principle, "My country, right or wrong"?

REAGAN: I think we have to believe it in the sense in which it was spoken. This doesn't mean that you can't have dissent. This means that, if we are to have a government, when the government in the name of the people takes a position, such as in a conflict, I think then we the people must support that country. We can't have a country in which we decide if the country is actually taking an action, legally and legitimately, that engages us in combat or in conflict. We may disagree, and we may continue to persuade our government to change that course, but we can't have the people deciding which wars they'll fight. We can't

—once you've taken a course. This is what "my country right or wrong" really refers to and what it means.

Suppose in other words that the anti-Vietnam demonstrators are wrong. Suppose our government and I happen to believe it is right in putting us in the position we're in. I think that it is to our national interest to be fighting where we're fighting because I think once you ask men to fight and die, then you unleash your military, your full national power to end that conflict as quick as possible. Now, we have to assume that government has access to much more information than the people, and that's particularly true under this Administration which has shown a reluctance to let the people have all the information; so government has made a decision based on our national interest on the belief that in the defense of this country, it is vital that we carry on this conflict in Vietnam. Some people without access to this same information are protesting vehemently and even to the point of now advocating literally help to the enemy and advocating that young men should refuse to fight for their country. What if these dissenters are wrong? And what if they succeed by their pressure in making this country withdraw from this position and then the course of history reveals that the government was right? It's the same situation we were in. Strangely enough the same people were on the opposite side in the days of Hitler, when your own country was holding a torch aloft in the world and trying to convince all the rest of the world that the world's safety depended on stopping the advance of Hitlerism and the isolationists in our own country wanted to say it's none of our business, why don't we stay home and not get involved. Well, I think if we look back on history now, we realize never has a war been so morally right, if war can be morally right. Never has there been a force that needed to be stopped as much as the

forces of Hitler needed to be stopped. But what if the isolationists had prevailed? Fortunately, they didn't. Now, it
would seem to me that some of these people who are taking a course—not the McCarthy course, who is, as I say,
literally presenting his case to the people and asking them
to weigh it—the other people who are burning draft cards
and trying to stop draft centers and stop troop trains and
communicate with the enemy, these people are taking a
terrible gamble.

FROST: I suppose they would say that their argument
is: what if the government is wrong?

REAGAN: Yes, but then we're asking for anarchy, aren't
we? We have to assume that while government does make
mistakes, government does have access to more information
than anyone else, and therefore we have to assume that
unless and until they can prove government wrong and
prove it legitimately in legitimate debate, not in curbing
these actions—it's like people arguing about whether to put
out a fire in the house while the house burns down.

FROST: Yes, but I think if government is wrong, if
government doesn't know best, it doesn't necessarily mean
anarchy, does it? A government can be completely wrong
without harming society totally, can't it?

REAGAN: Yes, as long as the government is not a dictatorship, as long as the government is such as the enlight-
ened Western nations have and certainly our own country
has, where there is a legal and legitimate channel for dissent for the people to make their will known, to question
government, to force government to explain.

FROST: In the light of the current conflicts in the
world, how would you today define the word Communist?

REAGAN: Well, generally within the context of Marx-
ism. The belief in a single party system, which means a

48

form of totalitarianism. It is the belief in government ownership and denial of the right of ownership to the individual. Generally, it denies the right of the individual. It downgrades the idea that the highest purpose of man is to grant freedom to the individual. It would make us all cogs in a well-oiled machine. In a way, it's very similar to the socialism of Hitler, who said that the only importance of the individual is his service to the state.

FROST: Would you say there's any basic difference between a communist dictatorship and a fascist dictatorship?

REAGAN: No, Nazism meant National Socialism, and there were various degrees and interpretations of it, much as we vary and differ in degree in our Judeo-Christian worship, with our many denominations, but all with a basic and underlying principle.

FROST: There can, I presume, be benefits. Are the Cubans better off now than they were under Batista, for instance?

REAGAN: Well, no. I am not perhaps a competent authority on Cuba, but strangely enough, Cuba was one of the more advanced countries of that kind. While certainly Batista was not an ideal ruler and certainly this country of ours could have used its economic power to make things better for the people, if you check you will find that in all Latin America, the Cubans had the highest standards of living. Their economy was broader based. They had wider distribution of the benefits of their society; many statistics bear this out: the number of homes with phones, with utilities, and so forth, per capita earnings, and this evidently isn't true now under Castro. It's possible by taking from the many, perhaps, he has placed a floor that might be something above the lowest we're allowed to have, and yet there's no real guarantee of that.

FROST: I'd like to come now, if I could, to the whole area of leadership. You must have thought about it a great deal. How would you define leadership?

REAGAN: Well, I suppose I automatically think of it now in terms of public office, of what not just an individual but a government should exert. I think the leadership must be dedicated to the principle of making decisions, to the best of its ability, on the basis of what is right or wrong and not on the basis of what is politically expedient. I think leadership requires taking a position even if that position is going to be highly unpopular. Your country has one of the greatest examples in modern times of that. Winston Churchill, who had the courage not to stand up and make political promises to his people, but said I promise you only blood, sweat and tears; and a Winston Churchill who rallied the people of England when invasion seemed imminent and the army had been lost at Dunkirk, or at least their materiel, and when he went before the people, he said, all right, we will fight them in the streets, every hedgerow—this man gave us so many examples of leadership. His appeal to Britain at the time when the philosophy of appeasement was widespread, and he pointed out, probably better than chapters and chapters of essays have ever proven or pointed out, the fallacy of appeasement.

FROST: This is a tremendously big question. What would you say at root that people are on earth for?

REAGAN: Well, of course, the biologist I suppose would say that like all breeds of animals, the basic instinct to reproduce our kind, but I believe it's inherent in the concept that created this country—and in the Judeo-Christian religion—that man is for individual fulfillment; our religion is based on the idea not of any mass movement, but of individual salvation. Each man must find his own salvation; I would think that our national purpose in this country—

and we've lost sight of it too much in the last three decades —is to free, to the limit possible within law and order, every man to be what God intended him to be.

FROST: And is there one historical character that you admire, feel more in sympathy with than any other?

REAGAN: One historical character?

FROST: Yes.

REAGAN: Well, of course, the one above all is the man whose simple teachings in a three-year span between the ages of thirty and thirty-three set down rules which if we had the courage to follow them would solve all the problems of the world today. The Prince of Peace, the man of Galilee.

FROST: My last question—it's a long way ahead, I'm glad to say—but how would you like to be remembered, what would you like the first line of your obituary to say?

REAGAN: Oh—oh, I don't know. That's a terribly difficult question. How do you not sound pontifical? I suppose nothing more than he tried and did his best.

Vice-President Hubert H. Humphrey

DAVID FROST: It's always a curious experience to read about yourself in the papers. I was wondering, do you recognize the picture of yourself in the press, or is there something you think the press leaves out? Are they accurate about you?

VICE-PRESIDENT HUBERT H. HUMPHREY: Well, I suppose that everybody is very subjective about himself. One of the limitations, I think, of the press is they really don't have time frequently to get to know you as you are as a private citizen, and each man is both private and public. Now, that doesn't mean you have a split personality, but your private attitudes and your private conduct and your private mannerisms in a sense condition your public life as well, and to really know a person you have to know him in depth, not only what's on the periphery, the skin of the man, but you have to know the bone and the sinew and the heart and the spirit of the man.

FROST: And if there is someone who only knew you as a public figure and got to know you privately, what would surprise them the most?

HUMPHREY: Oh my, that's hard to say. Well, I guess most people know that I like a great variety of people. I really enjoy a wide variety of acquaintanceship, and I get a cultural enrichment, so to speak, out of it, at least a spiritual enrichment out of it. I like prize fighters, for example; as a group they're very interesting. People in the art world and in the theatrical world—many of them are very, very generous. Sometimes they're very eccentric. You find people like the laboring people of our country, the working people. You find them with their very solid attitudes. There is a profundity even in simplicity, if you know what I mean. They're basic and yet, at the same time, they seem to be very open and very direct. I like children. I like them very, very much. In fact, when I get plain down, you know, tired and weary and discouraged, if I can walk out on the streets of Washington and see the school children and just visit with them, I find them really beautiful and attractive and interesting. They're bright-eyed, and they make you feel good. It's sort of like tonic. I do tire at times of adults. I guess we all do.

FROST: Looking back subjectively at your own career, what would you say thus far is the achievement that you're most proud of?

HUMPHREY: I suppose it might be that day in 1948 when I stood before the Democratic Convention and asked my political party to take a stand on the basic issue of our time and the basic issue of all time, human rights; and then we spelled it out, because the principle most people embrace, but the specifics of how to implement the principle was what was needed. I was a young man in politics and not known as a national figure. I was mayor of my city. I had practiced what I was preaching. It wasn't as if it was something I just decided to do at a convention. I knew that what I was talking about would work. I knew it made for a better city, and I was sure it would make for a better America, and I hoped that it would make for a better

Democratic Party. I felt that the time had come when the Democratic Party had to take its stand, and I argued the case against the majority of the resolutions committee for a strong and effective and clear and unmistakable stand on the whole issue of civil rights.

FROST: And looking at the impact that speech had then and the degree to which people in the South in the Democratic Party therefore went in their own direction in 1948 and now looking at the fact that you find yourself the choice for the next Democratic President of the Southern Governors, do you sometimes pinch yourself to see if it's true?

HUMPHREY: No, I feel that a man in public life ought to be an educator and a persuader. This is his first duty, to teach, to educate, to persuade, to convince, to develop a public attitude and a public opinion. I put over twenty years in it, and when I go into the Southern states and find Southern governors and Southern leaders that will support me—they don't agree on everything. They may think I go too far one way or not far enough another way, but when I find acceptance, I feel a real reward, not so much the reward only of their support, but the reward of the change that's taken place. There has been a tremendous change taking place in America. It's come so fast that most people have even missed that it happened. All they see is the turbulence that's with it, but there is a basic change of attitude and a basic change of social institutions in America. It's been almost like a revolution. It's been a peaceful revolution in the main, and it's happened in the South, just as it's happened in the North.

FROST: If, in that sense, the South has come toward you, has there been a similar change in you? Have you moved toward them in some way?

HUMPHREY: Oh, I'm sure that I've changed. I hope so.

When you're young you're very quick and you're sometimes a bit intolerant in your new-found knowledge. You are what we call brash and sometimes a little bit unforgiving. You think you're so right, and you don't wait, frankly, to find out that the other fellow may have a point of view. I'm sure that I've been guilty of all of those sins.

FROST: But when you look at what you said in '48, do you think on the one hand, ooh, I wish I hadn't been as brash or whatever then, or do you feel, oh, I wish I could see things as clearly now as I did then?

HUMPHREY: No, I have no regrets at all about what I did in 1948. I'm very proud of it. In fact, that was just the opening of the door, and we haven't really marched out into the full sunlight of full opportunity and equal rights and human rights. We're beginning. That door is opening more and more. More sunshine is coming into American life, and I see it coming all across our country. What we tried to do then helped develop what my aim is, namely, one citizenship in this country. I have worried about that we might have two Americas, the America of the affluent and the poor, the America of the white and of the black. The separate but unequal societies, as our commission on civil disorders said, but I don't believe that's inevitable. See, I believe that all of these things are manageable. I believe with effort and determination and conviction and program and courage, you can change these things. I believe in the capacity of the human being to shape history, to mold events, to create events and not just to be the victim of history or events.

FROST: Is there any episode in your career that you'd like to rewrite?

HUMPHREY: Oh my, I suppose there'd be several that I would like to do all over again. I doubt that I did a very good job, for example, in 1960, when I was in the Presidential primaries. I don't believe I was well enough organized in my whole effort. I doubt that I had the feeling in myself that I could do the job, and I think I rationalized my endeavors there more than I should have, but that's past. I don't spend much time worrying about those mistakes of the past, except to say, well, we have to do better the next time that we try it. I would imagine that there were times that a person wished that he stood a little more firmly, a little more openly.

FROST: For instance what?

HUMPHREY: Oh, during the days of the McCarthy era, the Joseph McCarthy period, I opposed Mr. McCarthy's attitudes. I opposed his tactics. I felt that America was going through a very unwholesome, degrading experience, and sometimes I feel that I should have stood up more strongly against him, but I was literally fighting for political survival and even though I voted against him and I took my knocks from him and his supporters, I think I could have been a little braver during that time.

FROST: It's a word to be used sparingly, I suppose, but how many great men are you conscious of having met?

HUMPHREY: I think it's very difficult as a contemporary to decide a man's greatness or lack of it because most of us are so busy that we don't have the time for thoughtful analysis and proper perspective, but some people are just obviously that way. The former Governor of New York, Senator Herbert Lehman, was a great man even when he came to the Senate. He had proven it. He had this quality of public integrity as well as private integrity that generates trust and confidence. You never needed to doubt that what he was doing was because he believed it with a depth of conviction. It never was for a particular political maneuver; that sort of a man, I believe, is essential in a free society. Paul Douglas, the Senator from Illinois—I didn't always find myself in agreement with Paul Douglas, but he was a tower of strength. A really brave man. Maybe at times people didn't think his political judgment was all that it should be, but there's one thing you can be sure of, that the man was a strong character, a great character, of moral principle —well, he was another one of the giants of politics. I believe that those two I could characterize in that manner without being extravagant.

FROST: It's difficult when you're close to people, of course. Would you call President Johnson a great man?

HUMPHREY: Yes, I would. His greatness is in an entirely different area. His greatness is in the knowledge and the techniques of government and understanding the big issues. Every President, of course, is an individualist. Each organizes his Presidency in a different manner. They're more or less like great conductors of great orchestras. You can have the same orchestra and bring a new conductor in each week and you get different music because the conductor has a way of instilling a spirit in that musician, even though the score that he reads from and the instrument that he plays are identical. I think that President Johnson's greatness also is in his tremendous dedication to the forward development of this country. He's not a radical, but he is a sincere progressive and he's a prudent man.

FROST: There are rumors around naturally about there being at some stage a sort of "draft Johnson" movement this year—you'd have to have very mixed feelings about that.

HUMPHREY: No, I wouldn't have any mixed feelings at all. If the Democratic convention felt that the President wanted or—I know he doesn't want it—that he should have the nomination, and if it was within the President's means to take on that responsibility again, I wouldn't have any mixed feelings. I think he's been a good President, and I feel that if he can achieve what his goals are, namely an honorable and genuine peace in southeast Asia and the unity of our country, or at least the reduction in the divisiveness that appears evident in our country, and that those great achievements would merit any reward and any support that the convention could give to him. I feel that if the President is not going to stand for election—and I'm sure he is not because he isn't one to play with words, or to play with emotions, or to play with the politics of his nation—I feel that if he is not to stand for election, then I have an obligation in a sense to do so and a right to do so, and I have a desire to do so.

FROST: In one book about you, he was quoted as saying that he thought you and he agreed on about ninety-five per cent of things. Would you say that's a fair percentage?

HUMPHREY: Yes, I would surely say so. He's been a very great teacher for me. All the good intentions in the world have little avail in government unless you know how to put them into effect; there are many good men, but men of effectiveness, of competence, of professional skill, ability, and this fine art of democratic government are few and far between. Just to have a good statement, a good heart, a good spirit, vital yes, but it takes something more than that to get a good government and good policy.

FROST: In what way will you expect—would you like—a Vice-President to be? I mean, if a Vice-President, for instance, working under you as President, disagreed on the grounds of conscience with what you were doing on a policy, would you expect him to speak out, or what?

HUMPHREY: I would expect him first to speak to me so that we could talk it out, hopefully reason it out; but I've always believed that there is a higher authority than legal authority, and I think a man's conscience is indeed that higher authority. If it was a fundamental, basic cleavage,

I would expect that that man would feel obligated to at least speak out; whether he would carry on a vendetta, or a political struggle, is another matter. I know that's the way I would feel. I feel that the first thing that a Vice-President owes to the President is his loyalty, and I believe that before he ever has any disagreement with the President publicly, if he were to have one, he has a solemn obligation to try to work it out privately. If it is a matter of conscience, and that word is loosely used these days, I regret to say, but of great deep spiritual involvement, then a Vice-President can do one of two things. Either keep his own counsel and bide his time, or he can speak out on the basis that it is more than he can take or endure.

FROST: Clearly you haven't had one of those fundamental—

HUMPHREY: Not at all. To the contrary. I believe that President Johnson will be known in history as having been responsible for some of the major breakthroughs in the social life and the social conditions of America and breakthroughs for the better.

FROST: You, of course, have a very different attitude from many of the candidates on the subject of the current American malaise, in the sense that most people talk about America as being ill. You're not so sure there is a malaise, are you?

HUMPHREY: In fact, I'm quite sure there is not. I'm sure there is a concern in America. There is ferment. There is change. There are difficulties and troubles, but I don't consider that basic sickness. I think it's a nation that is growing up, maturing.

FROST: Would you say basically then that America has been off course in the last few years?

HUMPHREY: No, I think it's been charting a new course, but it's a part of the continuing course of American history. I believe that we're in an era of emancipation. I believe this is what will characterize the second half of the twentieth century. This is not merely emancipation here in the United States for some of our people who have been deprived and who have not enjoyed all the blessings and all the privileges and responsibilities of full citizenship. I think you see it around the world. It doesn't come smoothly. There's never been basic change in history that came quietly. Freedom is not easily bought, and it comes really on the installment plan, you know. You don't get it all in one package. It comes time after time, and there's always a new area of freedom, a new dimension of freedom, and I think we're beginning now to see what we call participatory democracy. It isn't good enough to have government for the people. You have to have government *by* the people and that means right down to the basic decision-making processes of your democracy. As a matter of fact, I think tyranny has a terminal disease. I really do, and I think it's just a matter of patience and the perseverance and the mobilization of resources to get the job well done.

FROST: Senator McCarthy's supporters claim in their posters that, as a result of his campaign for instance, Our Children Have Come Home. Do you believe his campaign's brought them home, that they've never been away, or that they have yet to come home?

HUMPHREY: Oh, I think that in many ways Senator McCarthy's campaign has been very constructive. I believe that he did help involve young people in a constructive purpose. Now, we have some disagreements over some matters of policy, particularly on foreign policy, but that is really relatively unimportant. What's most important is that the involvement of people, young or old, is a constructive involvement. It's an involvement to try to make the changes peacefully, orderly, through the processes of democratic government, for redress of grievances, not in the streets, but rather in the meeting halls, through petitions, through elections, through the power of the ballot, and the power of the idea, and I think that the campaign that Senator McCarthy has launched has made a distinct contribution to that. I hope I can make one, too.

FROST: Senator Kennedy's too?

HUMPHREY: Yes, I think so, but Senator Kennedy has had a different appeal, to a younger group. I don't want to downgrade anybody's endeavor. I think what Senator Kennedy has been able to do is to recite quite precisely some of the great needs of our society, but I must say in all candor that I believe that Senator McCarthy has made a very timely entrance into the political scene. Now, whether that entrance will lead him to success only time can tell, but I know this, that he's a teacher at heart and he has been able to bring students around him so that they're active in a constructive cause. They're active for a purpose and for a man and for ideas. I think that's good.

FROST: At root, what would you say that people are on earth for?

HUMPHREY: They're on earth for two purposes. First, to make the most out of what they have in themselves. As we put it, to develop the great latent talents, the spiritual and the physical and the intellectual nature of man, and then to do that in a manner that is helpful to your neighbor, because while you must in one sense have your individualism, you must have your own dignity, your own character and your own being, you have to remember that you do not live alone. A man is not an island unto himself. He must always keep in mind that as he seeks his independence and his own liberty; he also must remember that he's a member of the human family, that he is an interdependent man and that he must live in a spirit of cooperation; ultimately the purpose of man's life on earth is to do good works and at first do it with himself to make himself a better person, to develop all the capabilities and the abilities that he has and then to use that, not only for self, but for one's neighbor.

FROST: One last question. It's a long way ahead, I'm delighted to say, but how would you like to be remembered—what would you like the first line of your obituary to say?

HUMPHREY: Well, as I think of it in these days, I'd like to be in a sense a sort of a healer.

FROST: Healing demands medicine. What's the basic medicine?

HUMPHREY: Well, I think we've been discussing that a good deal. It requires first of all a knowledge of one's self, trying to make something of one's self and a recognition that you do not live alone, that every right you have brings with it a responsibility, that every privilege you have carries with it a duty, that every luxury you have carries with it a burden. I think when people begin to balance it out and understand that they are not put on this earth just for their own self-indulgence, that they're here for a purpose of building a society—we call it a great society in America—a good society, a society of free men, well, I think that that's the ultimate purpose we have in mind.

The Hon. Harold Stassen

DAVID FROST: Governor Stassen, how would you define leadership?

HAROLD STASSEN: Leadership? Leadership is that quality that would cause people to move by their own decisions in a direction that is pointed out by the leader and agreed upon by the people.

FROST: And since you're standing as a candidate for the Presidency, this is a quality you feel that you have?

STASSEN: I feel that I have been able to exercise some of that at times, and, of course, the whole process is a continuing one.

FROST: What unique qualities would you say that you've got to offer as a candidate for president?

STASSEN: Well, my priority objective of building for peace. In other words, this from college days literally has been the number one aim. This is what led me into the political arena originally. I've never been one who has sought office for the sake of office. In fact, as you know, I resigned from the governorship and from the chairman of the governors to go on active duty in World War II, but the matter of how do you move this country and the peoples of the world in the direction that you feel

63

will build for peace, peace with freedom and with justice, means more and is more an intense factor in my life than the average individual.

FROST: How much have you changed? For instance, have you changed your attitude toward Richard Nixon since 1956, when you wanted him to be left off the ticket.

STASSEN: No, I've always recognized from actually very close experience that both Richard Nixon and Lyndon Johnson think differently than I do, you see. They—by nature—they think in the hard, tough line approach, and it is that hard, tough line that I am so deeply convinced leads to war and expanding war and can lead to the most tragic of wars. So I have basically opposed this hard, tough line, and I have rather advocated and tried to interpret what I would describe as the fair, firm line. See, I believe it should be fair even to the most extreme political opposition, that there is still a basic inner philosophy that you need to follow to be fair and, consequently, firm. There's a difference in my view between a firmness or this hard, tough line, and, consequently, I've always been much more restrained on triggering American troops into action, or sending American bombers into action. This, of course, now these last three years, has brought me into a sharp disagreement with the Johnson-Nixon approach to Vietnam.

FROST: You talk of Johnson as President. Now, at one time, you were spoken of as a future President. What do you think was the turning point in your elective career and what was the moment at which fate decided—perhaps it will now decide again—fate decided that you wouldn't continue at that time on the Presidential route?

STASSEN: Well, no one moment. You see, actually it's a continuing process, and I was well aware when I decided that if you're going to work for peace as you see it, that it would mean a matter of downs as well as ups and that you must persist and be patient and try to get through with your ideas. Of course, in that broad context, you see, having taken a part in drafting the original charter and signing it for the United Nations and in other movements that have come through significantly in the Eisenhower Administration, from my viewpoint, I consider that it's a winning life I'm leading, and the matter of experiencing some political defeats must be anticipated. That's a part of it.

FROST: But this has not got through to people that it's a winning life that you're leading. They just notice the defeats. They don't notice the man of peace thing.

STASSEN: Well, some do.

FROST: How is it a winning life?

STASSEN: Because of the very participation in establishing a United Nations, and now I'm gradually building up the awareness that you need now to modernize and strengthen that United Nations. You need to rewrite it.

FROST: But what would you refer to in the last ten years since you left administration? What would you point to that you've achieved in the last ten years?

STASSEN: Well, for one thing, of course, the limited nuclear test ban. You see, I worked with President Kennedy toward that, following through from the beginnings we made.

FROST: How did you work with him?

STASSEN: By direct talks and by correspondence and then by helping to mobilize support among the Republican Senators to ratify the treaty and from following through in talks with General Eisenhower who was then retired President that he would also join in the support of these constructive moves, and of course, encouraging some of these young men that I think have the right philosophy.

You know, like John Lindsay who was a Congressman and now Mayor of New York and Mark Hatfield who was a Governor and now Senator, encouraging these men as they stand up for what I believe are the very basic elements in the search for peace.

FROST: But, what was the worst moment you've had in politics thus far, the moment you'd most like to rewrite?

STASSEN: The worst moment? I think it's difficult to say, but I would say the worst moment was when I was unable to move the policies of the Eisenhower Administration during the Hungarian crisis. In other words, as that came up, I was so convinced that if we took an initiative right then to set up Hungary separate, to in effect give a way for Russia to let Hungary become independent like Austria, that we would move through and make real progress, but I could not get that policy sold at that time, and I felt there would come, you know, the tragic response of bloodbath.

FROST: What would you say in your career, is the most memorable phrase you've ever coined or created, that most put its finger on a situation?

STASSEN: I think that the phrase that I used very early that "he who lights the fires of racial or religious intolerance, lights the fire underneath his own house." I think this expressed the basic philosophy and carried through—this was in the very, very early days.

FROST: When did you first feel the desire to become President of the United States?

STASSEN: Well, this you may have difficulty in understanding, but I've never had a desire to be President of the United States, but I have had a very intense desire or rather conviction to move the country and the world on the basis for permanent peace.

FROST: But you talk so well about things you care about. It seems to me, looking at it from a distance that the one thing that perhaps holds back your campaign is that you do stand as a candidate for President because people don't talk about Harold Stassen, the man with the right views on peace. They talk about the Harold Stassen the man who loses all the time. Don't you think that these sorts of campaigns hinder your basic campaign, rather than help it?

STASSEN: Well, I've thought of that question, but actually your views begin to be, you know, publicized and understood in the way in which you feel you need to build for peace by being right in the political arena in this country. If you do not test your views in the politi-arena, they are substantially ignored in the real action so that you have to raise the issue.

FROST: But if you test them and they're so decisively rejected, surely that doesn't help?

STASSEN: When the others begin to adopt views and move in your direction then you sometimes have the impact in that way, you see.

FROST: You think that's happening?

STASSEN: Oh, it is.

FROST: They're moving in your way.

STASSEN: It has in previous times too, you see.

FROST: But you think now in '68 they're moving your way?

STASSEN: That's right. I believe that the basic objection that I've had that we should not endeavor to get an American war answer in Vietnam, that there cannot be an American war drive answer and that we must instead stop the bombing, de-escalate, quiet down the war, and move through the United Nations for having both Vietnams come into the United Nations membership, to move for United Nations solutions, to move to win the people instead of trying to kill our way—this is beginning to come through.

FROST: But I mean, I can see how that proves that you were right all along and that now people are seeing what should be the solution, but has your campaign had anything whatever to do with them seeing that?

STASSEN: I believe so, yes. In other words, I believe that the communication has come from the stand and on meeting the counter arguments. The dialogue and discussion in this country centers upon the political arena, and you have to step into it and argue it through and debate it through if you're going to move the people and the country into action.

FROST: How would you define an un-American activity?

STASSEN: Well, I wouldn't be engaged in such a description. See, I've never gone down that road, so to speak. As I said earlier, you know, America is a totality and I would say, you know, anything that's done within America is a part of America.

FROST: Do you believe in the principle, "My country, right or wrong"?

STASSEN: No, I do not. I believe that in a free society, in a society that has the moral principles that should underlie each society in the modern world, that the people constantly have to play a part in judging the actions of their own country; and this in fact is a part of the great change of the nuclear age, that it was always a luxury to have a narrow nationalism, but now it can lead to a holocaust, and we need to lift the thinking, to think of the well-being of all mankind.

FROST: And how would you like to be remembered? What would you like the first sentence of your obituary to say?

STASSEN: "He laid the foundation for a lasting peace."

FROST: That's a magnificent phrase. Tell me, as you look back at your life and as you look back at all you've struggled to do, when you look back at quotes like, "He's the man for 1944," or "Put your money on him as a future American President," and other things that the press said many years ago, what's your overwhelming feeling? Is it a slight sadness that that didn't come true?

STASSEN: No, no. You see, I live for the things to accomplish in the future, and I have a dimension of having taken part in originating the United Nations and in originating some of these other basic moves—"Atoms for Peace" and of the development of limitation on nuclear testing and the beginning of helping and backing President Kennedy in a bipartisan sense on the Peace Corps approach which tends now to get pushed back.

FROST: These are all great achievements, but now, when one reads through as I've done, the press clippings, one comes up all the while against phrases like, "holding press conferences in hotel hobbies where the potted palms outnumber the reporters." Don't you feel sad when you read things like that?

STASSEN: No, I recognize it as a part of a time in which your political influence is at a low ebb and you simply carry on. You know that when you're battling for basic principles on very major issues that at times you must suffer defeats and that you need to persistently follow through and also endeavor to encourage other young men to come forward and carry on.

FROST: Don't you feel now at this point that your political fortunes can only go to a lower ebb?

STASSEN: No, as a matter of fact, they've turned up somewhat already, and no one knows what the future holds, of course.

FROST: Do you rule out the idea of the Presidency in '68.

STASSEN: No, well, I have always said that I never close off future options of decision, but that I will endeavor to make the decisions on the basis of what will best advance peace.

FROST: And in ten, or rather twelve years' time, will you still be here running for President?

STASSEN: Well, that's a matter of God's will, of course. It's a matter of what years of vigorous life one is granted and what happens in the political system of one's country, but I intend to continue to be active so long as God does give me life.

FROST: And how do you know what's God's will?

STASSEN: Well, no one could ever be positive. You endeavor to interpret your basic religious convictions into the way in which you lead a life and the way in which you meet an issue, having drawn on the moral basis of life; but no one can ever say that you're absolutely sure that you correctly understand it. You search for it. You work on it, but you also must humbly realize that no one can be dogmatic as to attaining it or knowing it.

The Hon. George Wallace

DAVID FROST: Governor Wallace, if you had to pick one place to say that's the real, typical America, where would you pick?

GEORGE WALLACE: I don't know that I could pick any particular place and say that is the real America. I think the real America bounds all the way from the Canadian border to the Mexican border and from California to the east coast. I think we find America all over. I think basically the attitudes of the overwhelming majority of the people in this country are the same as far as fundamentals are concerned, and so I don't think any particular section has any monopoly on what's called America.

FROST: As far as Americans themselves are concerned, is there one sort of distinguishing characteristic that you'd say is very American?

WALLACE: Well, I think the people of our country are proud people. It's hard to pick out any distinguishing characteristic other than to say that I think by and large we are nationalistic. There is some attitude in Europe and other parts of Asia for a common market, for a united Europe, whereas in this country I think, with the excep-

71

tion of the few who are ultraliberal, we still are very nationalistic.

FROST: Everyone talks as though there's a great malaise in America. If there is some sort of malaise, what do you think is at the root of it?

WALLACE: I suppose all countries, because they're populated by human beings, have their problems. But we are progressing and moving forward in our country in the solution of problems that confront us in this century and in this year 1968, whereas we have confronted problems twenty and thirty years ago and solved them, so even though there are many things that we should strive to rectify and to change in our country, basically and fundamentally, this is a great nation and we're very proud of it. But I think one of the things of concern to the American people is the fact that we find a group in our country who have espoused the cause of strong central government, and we feel that this is not in keeping with the American Dream. It's not in keeping with the concept of those who brought our nation into being. We feel that in our country that we are centralizing the control over people's everyday lives in our national capital, and I feel that we're going to have a better country when we get back to letting the people in the respective political subdivisions which are the states—and I don't know whether you could call them a subdivision or not because the states of our nation actually formed our federal government. The federal government didn't form the states. They formed the federal government, and our constitution said that all power not delegated to the federal government is reserved to the states. Today we find our national, central government trying to take away the right of the people of Pennsylvania and of Alabama and of California to run their purely domestic democratic institutions.

We're going to have to get away from that because our government has enough problems in the foreign field delegated to them under the constitution without trying to run every phase and aspect of people's lives by controlling their domestic institutions.

FROST: Nevertheless, this agitation about the state having more rights does usually come up in connection with the issues involving the Negro. I mean, it doesn't come up concerning air pollution or oil depletion. It usually comes up in areas where a local state would like the Negro to have fewer rights.

WALLACE: Well, of course, your conclusion is erroneous when you say it comes up because people want the Negro to have less rights. I think that one of the great distortions throughout the world is the fact that people in our region of the country do not want people because of race to have the rights guaranteed to all citizens under our constitution. The crux of the matter is that the people in our region of the country, the Southland, applied common sense and logic to the amount of race relations, and we had a slow evolutionary process in which we had peace and tranquility unlike that existing any place in the world where there were people of opposite races; and now we find what I call the pseudointellectual elite cult who sit in their ivory towers and look down at the average man on the street and tell him that I must tell you about race relations. I must tell you where your child can go to school, where you can work. I can tell you what you can do with your business, or your farm. I must tell you who can teach your child and, of course, that has had race connotations also. We find that as a consequence, all of these pseudointellectual theories have been applied to race relations in our country. But where did we have the breakdown of law and order and the lack of peace and tranquility? We had it in Detroit. We had it in Los Angeles. We had it in Newark, New Jersey. We had it in New Haven, Connecticut. In Chicago, Illinois. We did not have it in those regions of the country where a common sense, logical approach to the problem of race relations had been applied. It's ironic in our country that people have called those of us racist who have tried to let local people work out matters involving race instead of someone a thousand or two thousand miles away in Washington. When you ask for that right to determine and solve matters at the local level, then the liberal says racist, fascist, hate monger. Yet evidently their theories have not worked because where they have applied their theories, we've had a complete breakdown of race relations, and we've had a complete lack of dialogue between the races. In our part of the country, we have better race relations, thank God, than any place above the Mason and Dixon Line, for which I am grateful. I have never made a statement in my life that reflected on anybody because of race or color. I don't ever intend to do so; but news media, television, radio, newspapers, magazines of the ultraliberal stripe, have written off every effort we have made in the field of race relations as being racist because it did not conform to their intelligentsia view of the matter of race relations.

FROST: At the same time, you must admit that on most of the occasions when you've taken issue on this question with the central and federal government, it's been because you wanted the Negro to have fewer rights written into various acts or bills. I was reading your book yesterday, *Hear Me Out,* the book of quotes, where you were talking about the civil rights bill and so on. You were opposing it because it was federal incursion into your territory, but in each case, you were opposing its provisions because you thought they went too far, weren't you?

WALLACE: No, sir, I didn't oppose the Civil Rights Bill because of wanting to hold back any right to anybody because of race or color. The Civil Rights Bills are misnamed. The Civil Rights Bills are an attack not only upon local government, but they are an attack upon the property ownership system. They are an attack upon the free enterprise system. The Civil Rights Bill tells an industry who they can hire and who they cannot. They tell a home-owner what they can do with their property; the latest Civil Rights Bill would put you in jail without a trial by jury because you didn't want to sell or lease your property to someone that some bureaucrat thought you ought to sell or lease it to.

FROST: No, that's not quite true though, is it? It isn't quite as simple as that. All they're saying is that a person shouldn't say no to someone else solely on the grounds of race. They can still say no to them because they don't want to sell their house at that price or something like that.

WALLACE: I think that a person who owns property or a home-owner, the old adage that came from—I think from England—I think from where you came from—that a man's home is his castle. The common law of England looked upon a man's home as his castle, but now the government of the United States wants a law passed that will be able to put the king of the castle in jail because he didn't want to sell his home or lease it to someone. I think that you ought to be able to sell or lease your property to anyone that you want to, or decline to sell or lease to anyone you want to for any reason under the sun because it's your home and your property. I would be against a law that said you could not sell property to someone because of race or color, creed, religion, or national origin; I'd be against that law just as strong as I am against one that says you must sell it to someone whether you want to or not.

75

FROST: You're saying that someone's home is their castle, but the whole point is they're moving out.

WALLACE: But it's their home. They have a right to move out and leave it vacant. They have a right to say we're going to sell it only to people with English accents. We have a right to sell it only to people with bald heads or blue eyes. We have a right to sell this property to only people who go barefooted, if that's what the home-owner wants to do.

FROST: Let me then ask the age-old question that's asked on this race issue. Would you let your daughter marry a Negro?

WALLACE: I don't even want to get into a discussion of that business. In fact, I don't even want to discuss the matter of race really, because the most important thing in our country is maintaining law and order. Race relations are going to work themselves out insofar as people are concerned. I'll put the question to you. Would you like for your daughter to marry someone of an opposite race, and I think that's a matter that will have to be left up—I don't believe in intermarriages of Negro and white—I'm candid and honest about it. I don't think it's good for either race. I think the races ought to remain intact. I think God made one race. He made another race, and that it ought to be that way, but if anyone wants to intermarry, that's their own business.

FROST: But you think it's not good for either race?

WALLACE: I think that it's not good for either race, that's right.

FROST: Because it does what?

WALLACE: Well, you see, that's one reason I don't even like to discuss these matters with you folks. All you want to do is talk about race. Now, you come from England, where you folks passed a law over there that you don't even let Asians come into the country.

FROST: Oh I know. We've got nothing to preach about.

WALLACE: I just don't even want to talk about race. I'm not even going to talk about blood lines. I'm just going to talk about the common-sense right of people in the States to determine the policies of domestic democratic institutions and let them decide those questions.

FROST: Yes, but you made a point; you must explain it. You made the point you think it's not good for either race. Why is it?

WALLACE: I think for obvious reasons, and I'm not going to discuss it any further. I'm not going to discuss it any further, that's all.

FROST: But the reasons aren't obvious.

WALLACE: I'm not going to give you any. I don't have to give any reasons for it. I just don't think intermarriage among the black and white races is good. Now, that's— you've got what you want.

FROST: Well, no, I don't particularly want to—

WALLACE: Well, I say I'm not going to discuss it any further.

FROST: Why, because it's irrational—

WALLACE: I just don't want to discuss it. I don't want to—you discuss it.

FROST: —or will come out as prejudice?

WALLACE: I just don't want because that's all you talk about is race, and that—I'm not a racist, and I'm not anti-Negro and every time I'm on a program of any sort whether they be Westinghouse, English, British, France, they want to talk about race and I'm just not going to—I don't have anything against anybody because of race, and that's all I'm going to say about it.

77

FROST: No, let me make it clear. I want to talk about God and the country and a great many other things, but the point is, you're usually so explicit and good in your explanations that it makes one rather mystified why this is one point you can't explain.

WALLACE: Well, I've mystified you now.

FROST: Ladies and gentlemen at home, you're all mystified. One last question on this subject and then we'll move on to the next while they're still mystified. Do you support or oppose the Ku Klux Klan?

WALLACE: I made the strongest speech against the Ku Klux Klan ever made in this state over statewide television in '58.

FROST: What one sentence from that would you quote?

WALLACE: I don't remember. It was a thirty minute speech, but all I can say is that that's not important either. There are not enough members of the Ku Klux Klan to count on your fingers and toes, and yet people make big issues about that organization when they ought to be talking about the Communist movement in our country that's advocating that it be burned down. In running for the Presidency, people are going to have to support me on what I stand for, and any organization that supports me doesn't mean that I support them. I don't know whether they support me or not. There's not enough of them to count in the first place; President Johnson received the support of the Communist Party in 1964, but he's not a Communist. He's an anti-Communist, and for me to say that he's a Communist because he was supported by the Communist Party would be ludicrous and asinine. So to say that I support some organization because some person supports me who happens to be a member would also be ludicrous and asinine. I do not advocate violence in the solution of any problem on the domestic scene. I do not advocate any campaign against anybody because of race, color, creed, or religion or national origin. I'm not like some of the liberals in our country. I believe there's a God and that he made all of us and that he loves all of us and that all people in this country, regardless of their race, are children of God. I do believe that, so as a consequence I've never run any campaign against anybody because of race or color, creed or religion or national origin; but the Ku Klux Klan is the most overblown issue in this country. The organizations in this country that we should be concerned about are the organizations advocating Communist victory in southeast Asia, who are advocating the burning and destruction of cities in our country.

FROST: How would you define the word Communist?

WALLACE: Well, of course, when you talk about the economic theory of Communism, I've read *Das Kapital* and the *Communist Manifesto*. Frankly, Communism is whatever totalitarian form those on the inside want to make it, whether it be in Bulgaria, the existing Hungarian regime, or Czechoslovakia, or over in China, but in Russia—but I'm thinking about the aggressive aspect of Communism. I'm talking about the economic theory. If people in Communist China want the economic theory of Communism, whatever that happens to be, they can have it. However they define it. They can have it, but their matter of trying to subvert the free governments of the world to military subversion, those are the things I oppose. So I say that anyone in this country who believes in the Communist enonomic theory and wants to advocate it and wants to elect people at the polls who will bring about such a theory, that's within the constitutional context and that is the way you change things in this country, if that's what you want. But to those on the college campuses who advocate Communist victory in southeast Asia, regardless of what the definition of Communism

is, they ought to be dealt with by the laws of this country
and they ought to be put in jail.

FROST: You say regardless of the definition. But you
haven't really defined what is Communist about—

WALLACE: —well, I don't exactly know what it is other
than to say that it's a theory in which the state owns and
operates and controls the economic lives of the people of
that particular country. State ownership, state control. That's
Communism to me.

FROST: That's socialism.

WALLACE: Socialism is just one step from Communism
in my judgment. There's not much difference in it. State
ownership and state control—

FROST: What's the step that's—

WALLACE: There's a step toward it. I don't know how
big a step it is, but—

FROST: When does a socialist become a Communist?

WALLACE: What's that?

FROST: When does a socialist become a Communist?

WALLACE: I couldn't tell you. I think that a socialist is
moving toward Communism and, of course, socialism is state
control, and so is Communism.

FROST: Governor, do you believe in the principle "My
country, right or wrong"?

WALLACE: Yes, I believe in my country right or wrong.
I believe we have a right to speak out against those actions
taken by our country that you consider wrong, but if you are
talking about involvement in southeast Asia, if you're talking
about Vietnam, there's much difference of opinion about
that; but as long as American servicemen are committed between life and death in southeast Asia, then I'm for standing
with them and they are my country while they are there.
Whether they should be there or not is not the question. As
long as they are there, then they're entitled to the total

commitment of the American people. And so whether they should be in Vietnam or not, I am still with the servicemen and hope we take whatever action is necessary to bring them safely back honorably. The first soldiers went in under the first Kennedy Administration and then escalated of course in the Johnson Administration, but I do stand with the servicemen, and right or wrong we should stand with them in southeast Asia.

FROST: Would you say that there's any difference between a Communist dictatorship and a Fascist dictatorship?

WALLACE: As far as the people in that particular country, there probably wouldn't be much difference. Nazism and Fascism in my judgment came from Communism's book. It's totalitarian, it's repressive, it destroys individual liberties and freedoms and the civil rights of the people—there are no civil rights in my judgment in a Fascist country, or in a Nazi country, or in a Communist country; but the only difference that I see is that those countries that might be Fascist today at least are not trying to subvert the governments of other countries in the world. Franco Spain—I'm not an admirer of Franco, but as long as he's friendly to our country and as long as he doesn't want to try to impose through military force and subversion and espionage and sabotage his philosophy upon the peoples of the adjoining countries or throughout the world, then they can have Fascism in Spain if that's what they want. That's not any business of the people of this country and not any business of anybody else.

FROST: You once said, again quoting your book *Hear Me Out,* that if you had the choice and you had to choose, you'd rather be a Fascist than a Communist. Why is that?

WALLACE: Well, I don't know why I said that and I don't know whether I said that or not, frankly. I've seen many quotes in newspapers throughout the country that I never made. I saw them in *Time* magazine that I've never made. I saw them in *Newsweek* magazine that I never made, so I don't know that I ever said that because it would be a very poor choice to have to choose between Communism and Fascism. They are both evil systems in my judgment. If I had to choose between Communism or Fascism—I'll amend my statement—I wouldn't choose either. I'd just be a nonchooser if that's all I could choose. I'd just stand mute and not choose either.

FROST: You were quoted in the book as saying that you'd choose Fascism because at least Fascists believe in God.

WALLACE: Well, I don't know whether I said that or not, and I don't know whether Fascists believe in God. I'm talking about maybe the people in Franco Spain. They have not outlawed the church in Spain. You can still worship in Spain. Is that not correct? Well, evidently then there is some connection with my statement in reality. In Communism they do not even recognize the existence of a Supreme Being.

FROST: You were talking about Communism being deliberately spread. A lot of people say Communism spreads, in fact, simply where there's poverty, discrimination, and lack of opportunity.

WALLACE: Those are the existing conditions that Communists take advantage of, and yet when they take over, there's more poverty and less opportunity than existed prior to when they took over. We have East Germany and West Germany as two examples of the existence of poverty after World War II, and yet we find that there's more poverty in East Germany today than there is in West Germany.

FROST: On the other hand, Cuba is said to be a better

country for Cubans now under Castro than it probably was under Batista.

WALLACE: No, sir, I don't agree. I think that Cuba—the Cuban people today—whenever you kill thousands of citizens in a bloodbath, do you mean to tell me that's better than anything? They didn't have that type of bloodbath in the other regimes prior to Castro. When thousands of Cuban citizens have had to flee to this country because of the danger to their life, when Cuba today, a nation that we freed in a war with Spain, and that traded with our nation, and whose economy was in better shape before Castro—to say that the Cubans are better off in my judgment is not a fact. I think they're worse off and the free world's worse off because of Castro.

FROST: As you look back through history, which historical character do you most admire, do you feel most in sympathy with?

WALLACE: Well, I don't know. I think that maybe Cicero was a good man, and I think maybe Moses was a great man and, of course, I think the life of Christ—I think I admire his personal life and—probably more than any other man in existence, but aside from talking about deity and Christ, I would say—of course, I have a high regard for George Washington, father of our own country, and many of those who founded our nation and wrote her constitution and the Declaration of Independence. Those are some.

FROST: Richard Nixon picked Abraham Lincoln. You wouldn't agree with him?

WALLACE: Well, Abraham Lincoln was a great man. I didn't agree with all of Abraham Lincoln's philosophies, and he was not always correct in some of the things he said about matters of the day, but had he lived, the

South would have been spared the vengeance of Reconstruction; one of the worst things that ever happened to the people of the South after the war was the assassination of President Lincoln. President Lincoln was a great man.

FROST: It's very difficult to summarize your feelings about politicians, but in what they've done in the last three or four years and as you've watched them, if you had to pick one single adjective to describe President Johnson, what one single adjective would you use to describe his Presidency?

WALLACE: I don't know. I certainly don't want to sound personal in my criticism of the President or Mr. Nixon or Mr. Rockefeller or Mr. Kennedy, or any of them, because I don't involve in personalities, but I think his administration could best be described by the expression "disliked."

FROST: And how would you, looking at Mr. Nixon's policies, how do you find them different?

WALLACE: Not enough difference to even discuss. I think that what he has advocated in the past and stood for on the domestic scene and otherwise parallel to almost the same thing that President Johnson stands for.

FROST: This is a tremendously big question—what would you say basically, Governor, that people are on earth for?

WALLACE: Well, of course, we are here because God wanted us to be here. Of course, I realize that it's sort of obsolete and outmoded to speak of God any more, especially in some liberal circles in our country and throughout the world, but I believe in the existence of a Supreme Being. Although it's hard to comprehend a powerful power omnipotent as God possesses, but what I cannot comprehend and what I do not know in my own mind or can rationalize or argue or develop logically, I bridge that gap with faith. I do believe that there is a Supreme Being and that he placed us here and that we do have a purpose in being here. I think one purpose is, of course, to deal with and treat our fellow man under what we call the golden rule, which is really a principle enunciated by Christ and that I feel that there's an after life.

FROST: You're a Methodist, and Methodists have got some wonderful hymns. Which is your favorite?

WALLACE: Well, I have many favorite hymns. I don't know exactly which ones at the moment, but I like "Rock of Ages"—that's a great one—and then the one "Abide With Me" and—but I think "Rock of Ages" is one of the finest of the hymns.

FROST: How does that go?

WALLACE: Well, I can't—I'm not a singer. I can't sing it for you, but—"Rock of Ages, cleft for me, let me hide myself in thee"—that's one of the first lines.

FROST: It takes us on really to a point that Governor Reagan was making when he talked about the loosening of morals in this country. What do you feel about those problems?

WALLACE: I think that the attitude now is that anything goes as far as what you write and what you say in public and what you say over the television, or radio, or what you say in the movies. I don't believe in censorship necessarily, but some of the films I see today are just not fitting for anyone to watch, and some of the books and literature sent through the mail; but, of course, our Supreme Court has held that you can send this type literature through the mail, but you cannot bow your head and say a simple prayer in a public school, thanking God for having blessed you. This is some of the pseudointellectual theories that the people in my country don't understand and are really one of the issues in the forthcoming Presidential race. The aver-

age man on the street just can't understand some of the
decisions of our courts that say that you can send any sort
of literature through the mail and write a long big opinion
that I can't understand—maybe they can understand it—
setting out reasons why, but then on the other hand they'll
write that it's unconstitutional to say a prayer which is so
simple, "God is good. God, we thank you for our food."
They prohibited that in lunchrooms throughout the country
under decisions of the court. You certainly shouldn't have a
Methodist prayer required to be prayed, nor a Buddhist
prayer, nor a Catholic prayer, nor a Protestant prayer, nor
a Jewish prayer, but common sense has separated church
and state and when people get up and say a simple prayer
in a public school, in my judgment, it's not unconstitutional.

FROST: How would you define today in '68, an un-
American activity?

WALLACE: How would I define what?

FROST: How would you define an un-American activity?

WALLACE: I would define an un-American activity as
some of these professors on some college campuses making
speeches calling for victory of the Communists over the
American servicemen in the name of free speech and academic freedom. We're going to destroy academic freedom
by our use of it, and no one has a right to call for Communist victory in this country while American servicemen
are being killed by Communists. You say, well, the war is
not declared. That's purely technical. I think that the Attor-
ney General of our nation ought to seek an indictment
against anyone in this country that makes a speech calling
for Communist victory, especially when it is printed in the
Communist press and boosts the morale of the Communists
in Hanoi. Anyone who advocates the overthrow of this government by force or violence is engaging in an un-American
activity, and any member of the Communist Party who

owes his allegiance to a foreign power such as American Communists do is engaged in un-American activities.

FROST: Of course, there have been in the last ten or fifteen years in American politics, two Senator McCarthys, Senator Eugene McCarthy and Senator Joseph McCarthy. Which of the two would you say has made the greater contribution to American life?

WALLACE: Of course Senator Joseph McCarthy was in existence a pretty good while ago, but Senator McCarthy was not far wrong in his attitude of the Communist menace in this country. We see it every day today. We see even now Dean Rusk and the President saying that there are Communists involved in the demonstrations. We knew that five years ago. Dean Rusk now says the same thing that Mr. McCarthy said some time ago. There were Communists involved in movements of this sort. So Mr. McCarthy may have been a little broad in some of his accusations, maybe, but in my judgment, the statement that Communism is a serious threat to the internal security of our country is a fact. Those who have advocated the burning of cities in this country and have helped to set them on fire have wound up the next week in Hanoi, Peking, and Moscow and Havana. Now, the average man on the street knows there is a connection even if the President's crime report doesn't see fit to so connect. Senator Eugene McCarthy, he makes a definite contribution because he has given a definite position. I do not agree at all with many of the pronouncements of Senator McCarthy—Eugene McCarthy—but he certainly has a right to run for the Presidency, and I respect his opinion and believe that he's honest in his convictions.

FROST: How would you like to be remembered? It's a long way ahead, I'm glad to say, but what would you like the first line of your obituary to say?

WALLACE: I don't know. I don't have any sense of history that evidently your question thinks I might have. Maybe the first line of my obituary: "Born August 25, 1919," and I'd like the second line of it to say "Died August 2040."

FROST: Looking ahead there are one or two people who think that you might hold the balance when the elections are all over.

WALLACE: I think there are more than one or two people who think that really, but—in our region of the country —although our candidacy is not regional, it's national—we are pretty solidified in the Southland, and we are going to determine some policies in national and international affairs in the next four years.

FROST: And if there came a moment where the two sides were deadlocked and you held the balance, with whom do you think you'd be able to make your solemn covenant?

WALLACE: Well, I have no idea, and the only reason I've talked about a covenant is because of questions projected in that fashion. That's purely hypothetical and very speculative, and I don't think it's going to come about. I think I can win the Presidency with at least a plurality of the votes and enough states to win a majority of the electoral vote; but if that came about, whoever gets the support that we would be able to throw to him or to that party would have to make a covenant to the American people and that covenant would have to be the embracing of most of the planks of our platform, not to me personally, but to the American people.

Mayor John V. Lindsay

DAVID FROST: If we could start, Mayor Lindsay, with a very wide question, what would you say is your ideal America, or your ideal for America?

MAYOR JOHN V. LINDSAY: Well, America is thought of, and I think of it, as a young country. It's a country which has constantly changing conditions and people, and that's a great virtue; so I like to think of America as a dynamic, fast-moving, high-pressure nation that is competitive and yet which has the sense and wisdom to preserve all values and traditions whenever they're discovered or whenever they're made. I see it also as a country of vast expanse. Each time I travel across it and around it, I'm always reminded how big it is and of its diversity.

FROST: If you had to pick one place out of this vast continent and say, "that's typical, that's the real America," where would you point?

LINDSAY: I think you'd take almost any suburban community these days. There was a time when that wasn't true, but now America is kind of a very large suburb into which the core cities are creeping, and then the suburbs are beginning to touch each other across the country. If you travel in an airplane from the east coast to the west coast and look out the window, you'd be amazed at the vast expanse of fields and mountains that are there with no people, but that is not what America is today. Whether you're in Arizona, or in Idaho, or Minnesota, or Wisconsin, or New York, you're going to find yourself most of the time in suburbia—kind of middle-class America, rather affluent and rather comfortable, but with growing pressures all around them.

FROST: What's the essence, would you say, of being American? Is there a characteristic that you'd say singles out Americans from other nationalities?

LINDSAY: That's a very difficult question. I describe an ideal American as one that is energetic and adapts to change, uses it, is competitive and hard hitting. I don't suggest that in a crass way. I'm trying to do it positively. I think Americans largely go at a less leisurely pace than most nationals of other countries that I know, whether you're talking about the European community or Asiatics. Americans really expect more in many ways which is both a virtue and a vice.

FROST: How is it a vice?

LINDSAY: I don't mean it pejoratively, and I don't mean it by way of high compliment either. It's a vice because there perhaps is a tendency to find it difficult to enjoy leisure. Americans are sufficiently impatient so that they find it difficult to develop the quality of leisure.

FROST: Yes, I agree about that. The very fact of being more ambitious and competitive at work means that Americans work better than the English, but their lives are less relaxing. In this year everybody is behaving as always happens in an election year, like doctors trying to diagnose the ills, and people will be talking about what ails America and agreeing that there's some malaise and so on. What is that malaise?

LINDSAY: I think as you approach national elections in the world today, you're going to get a good deal of discussion about a malaise that affects a nation. Your own country, Great Britain, certainly went through this during the turbulent period of Harold Wilson's election.

FROST: Oh, we've enjoyed a perpetual malaise.

LINDSAY: Your people preserve a wonderful sense of humor about—

FROST: We find we need it more and more!

LINDSAY: Here in the United States we're going through external and internal problems. The nation has discovered that it has a deep sickness like any country will discover in a portion of its society, and like any democracy it's got to get on with the difficult job of fixing it up.

FROST: How would you define that deep sickness?

LINDSAY: In our country, of course, it's the pressure of the cities. The urban problem has been growing, and the nature of the city is one that has not really been studied or figured out. The problem has largely grown since World War II actually. It's always been with us through the history of these great urban centers; but since World War II, it's had an impact around the whole nation as the result of years of neglect and absence of planning, absence of talent and techniques and systems and weak governmental institutional life at the local level. The result of all this has come to a boiling head in tensions and poverty and bad housing, all systems that have outlived their usefulness.

FROST: Is there any reason why it should have exploded so much now, or has it just been growing and this just happens to be the moment when it's boiled?

LINDSAY: Well, it's an optimistic sign that it has happened now because it's meant that people, particularly poor people which are mainly non-Whites, Negroes, living in the core city areas of the North and South, especially the

North now, from coast to coast have discovered—perhaps through greater knowledge through television, through other means—the importance of the problem themselves. They're hungry for entry into the mainstream. We're talking about many millions of persons for whom the American dream has meant very little, and the time has come to go through the sound barrier. Perhaps it's related somewhat to world change. This has an impact to some extent. I think attitudes among people, just like among nations, are very contagious.

FROST: When I was talking to Senator McCarthy about malaise, he was talking about a period during President Kennedy's rule when America was starting to get moving. Then there has been this period when things have come to a full stop under President Johnson. You would cite something much more specific than that. It is not to do with the atmosphere of leadership so much as to do with the problem of cities? This is the basis?

LINDSAY: I think that's one of the key bases. I'm sure that Senator McCarthy would have said that the war in southeast Asia has the major part to play in the unhinging of the country in so many respects, and he's right. It has had a role and a very important role, and there is a question of leadership without doubt at every level. But I do think that no matter who had been President, increasingly the tension in these cities which boiled over last summer into civil disorder in over fifty cities was bound to happen. It was stamped in history that this was going to happen, that it was almost inevitable the way things were going. Now, whether different leadership could have prevented it, or if President Kennedy had lived, it would not have been as virulent and as tense, I don't know. That's speculation.

FROST: How would you define leadership?

LINDSAY: Well, leadership has a tone to it. There's a

quality to it that must come through. I think that the person who will ultimately emerge as a leader of some power and direction is one that the people sense has within him an internal gyroscope that always brings him and therefore the institutions that he leads or commands back on to the course. What ultimately is needed is high quality and if you have men who have character, then you're going to find leadership. It sounds very old-fashioned, doesn't it, to look for character, but that's ultimately what it comes down to, I think.

FROST: To what extent can leadership in fact change the direction of a nation? Or to what extent can it only just follow the direction a nation's going?

LINDSAY: The old question—do men make history or history make men, and can men control their destinies by their acts?

FROST: Can you give one specific example of what you consider good leadership?

LINDSAY: Well, let me give the example of two recent Presidents. President Eisenhower I think definitely showed leadership in the problems of Europe and of the Near East. I think he showed leadership in his dealings with some of the more complicated international issues of the day. I think that President Kennedy began to show leadership in the short time that he lived as President in the area of civil rights and in the movement in this country that was committed to it. One must give him credit for the acceptance of the great march on Washington in 1963. One must give him, I think, credit for the poverty program.

FROST: To hear you talking about all of these people brings me to the thing that I sometimes find bewildering about the way people are identified in the two parties in America. I find it particularly bewildering in your case. Why are you really a Republican and not a Democrat.

Don't you in fact feel on most issues much closer to say McCarthy or Kennedy than you do to say Reagan, Nixon, or Goldwater?

LINDSAY: It depends on what the issue is you're talking about or how you're putting it. Many of the things I'm trying to do in the City of New York now have a great Republican background, tradition, and heritage. I would hope that my party would have the wisdom to capitalize on what is needed now. Decentralization, concentration on local government to make it more perfect, communication with people on the block, restructuring our institutions of government, and some of the quasigovernment ones in order to enable people to relate to government. Now, all of this has a high degree of concentration on the importance of the individual and the relationship of the individual to institutional life in his community and bring it down to the block level, or street level if you wish. It's highly Lincolnian in its approach.

FROST: But liberal Democrats would share that as much as liberal Republicans.

LINDSAY: Might, but the Republicans would have the higher claim on that as a philosophy if they used it and built on it and pushed it hard.

FROST: They'd have the first serial rights on it, you think?

LINDSAY: Yes, because this has been the tradition of the party in its beginnings and in its great periods.

FROST: Those are important issues, but nevertheless, not the ones that initially come to mind, and on a lot of major issues one could see you as easily in the Democratic Party as in the Republican. How would you conclude a sentence like: I could never be a Democrat because—?

LINDSAY: I can answer that by saying this: I saw the Democratic Party when I was in the Congress, and still see it, although life is changing so rapidly in the country that it's difficult to make flat statements, in the big cities of the North as a great collection of big city machines that were unchanging in their attitudes, monopolistic in their approach to life and to government. Now when I first became acquainted with political life and understood what it was all about, it was when Mayor Fiorello LaGuardia was the Mayor of this city. He was the first politician I ever met, shaking his hand. He was a Republican. He was against the machine. He was a man who was individualized and with the people. He read the funny papers to the kids and he went out to fires. He denounced wrongdoing, and he wandered around in his shirtsleeves. The bad guys were the cigar smoking, backroom, machine men. Then at the time I went to Congress, I could see that the institution was dominated by a different kind of special power system, and these were the men that had had longevity coming up through the Democratic Party in the South. They controlled the power levers in Congress and still do, and I saw this as the group that was fighting the things that I thought were important, the things that Mr. Lincoln began with the Republican Party which was civil rights and the rights of individuals. So in one part of the country I could see the individual being throttled by antilibertarian views. In another part of the country, I could see the individual being throttled by machine life. That was the Democratic Party and under those circumstances as a Republican, I felt and feel today far freer, far less trapped.

FROST: What you're saying is: if you were a good guy in New York, you had to join the Republicans—but somewhere else it might have been the Democrats?

LINDSAY: Well, the party of reform was the Republican Party in New York City and I find that around the country some of the bright young men that have been the reformers have been Republicans. This is true in the South now too.

FROST: Who would you say is your favorite historical character? Who do you feel most in sympathy with in history?

LINDSAY: Don Quixote. I've always had a fondness for a couple of your old Prime Ministers—Gladstone and Disraeli are two.

FROST: Which of the two?

LINDSAY: Interesting characters, both different. Disraeli was the guy that I wrote my thesis about when I was at the university, and I found him a fascinating study. Cromwell was another one. He wasn't a very decent fellow. He was a terrible old Puritan and killed people for his Puritanical ideals.

FROST: He was a Republican.

LINDSAY: Oh, was he? I thought he was—I would have thought he was another type! I was a great fan of Mr. Churchill. I was fortunate enough to be in London at the time of his funeral. I was actually there for another purpose but witnessed the whole business. It was a very dramatic occasion.

FROST: What about your own personal history? Is there one episode as you look back on your life thus far that you would like to rewrite?

LINDSAY: You mean something in my own personal history that I could rewrite?

FROST: Well, personal career, perhaps should we say. Is there some mistake, some unsaid word—

LINDSAY: Oh yes, I say things all the time I wish I hadn't said, and I don't say things I should have said. I never go through a press conference but what I immediately say—well, now, you should have done that entirely differently. I can't answer your question with something that is dramatic or so big. There are some small things and tiny things.

FROST: What sort of things?

LINDSAY: I wish very much that after the war was over and I'd gone back to see if I could pick up the educational stream where I'd left off, that I'd stretched it out. I wish I'd taken a year or two out to go abroad at some point in order to perfect at least one other language. I felt too much in a rush and did not do that, but I think that kind of thing was relatively minor.

FROST: In your political life, is there a decision you regret?

LINDSAY: In my political life? No, because the whole thing has been a fresh experience. I wish I had time to reflect on it more and to write some notes and to do some writing about it, because it would—if I told all—be quite a story.

FROST: What would surprise people most?

LINDSAY: Well, I don't know. I think things that surprise people most are relationships, people relationships—that really is the most trying part of government, I think. It's not the science of it. It's people relationships, and the more you discover that people are human beings, why the more you discover that they all have weaknesses and failures.

FROST: Which of your people relationships would surprise people?

LINDSAY: Would surprise people? Oh, I don't know. I think that the more you advance in this business in which I'm in, the more you discover that the personal relationship is in the last analysis critically important. You're dealing with big institutions and big stakes and lots of power, and yet the personal relationships can play a very, very majestic

97

role, an important role. When Mr. Churchill said that the Cross of Lorraine was the chief cross that he had to bear, meaning Mr. DeGaulle, he was talking about a very personal relationship. He wasn't talking about the French Government or the history of France or of the war or its aftermath or anything else. He was talking about a human being that he had a problem with, and that's increasingly, I think, the way you discover life is. To go back to the question you asked a little while ago, do men control their own destiny, the more you see of relationships between people, the more you discover that they just might be able to. Have you seen *Tiger at the Gates?*

FROST: No, I haven't.

LINDSAY: Because that's a discussion on the march of history indicating that war is inevitable and that it's uncontrollable and that men can't stop the march of events. It's the story of the Trojan Wars. His theory is that women begin it all, that men go to war because of women. Do you think that's true?

FROST: I don't know. History is supposed to march on men's stomachs rather than women's bodies. But perhaps great men can change things. Do you believe in the principle, "My country, right or wrong"?

LINDSAY: That's too simple.

FROST: How would you modify it?

LINDSAY: Patriotism is always a difficult thing because some people do the most outrageous things in the name of patriotism. Tacitus, I think, described patriotism as a healthy competition with one's ancestors.

FROST: That's a great definition. So to come back to it, how would you then modify the phrase, "My country, right or wrong"?

LINDSAY: Well, it's an impossible phrase. It lends credence to the notion that in free countries, in democracies, men have no control whatsoever over their destinies, and one would assume that if one's country was on completely the wrong track in a democratic system, that you'd change it.

FROST: And you would assume that is almost always possible?

LINDSAY: I think it's possible and indeed, it's got to be, this day and age, with hydrogen bombs around in various countries' arsenals.

FROST: Would you say that there is anything by definition different about the idea of a Fascist dictatorship and a Communist dictatorship?

LINDSAY: Again, to be overly simplistic about it, if that dictatorship should deny individuals fundamental rights, free speech, freedom to worship, freedom of communication, freedom to be free of the degradation of abject poverty, freedom to travel—if an individual is denied those basic rights, then to him there is no difference between Fascism and Communism.

FROST: And what about the difficult situation that emerges, let's say, in an emerging country where there is a country with a regime that is undemocratic but non-Communist, and the situation is one that if democracy came, the country would probably vote to go Communist. Do you think that that should be encouraged or what?

LINDSAY: In the long run, you have a healthier situation if free democratic institutions are there, even if the results to somebody else are not to his liking, but if there's a free secret ballot, in the long run you're better off. You may have a more hesitant government and you may not be able to accomplish quite as much in building blocks and the other things that you should want to do. Here I am the Mayor of the City of New York, and in my private moments I have to say to myself that it would be far better as far as I'm concerned if I were a dictator of this city and that we had no democratic institutions at all because we can't enjoy that luxury. Democracy is a bit of a luxury, and yet on second thought, I can't admit that because I know that even though I'm frustrated by the checks and balances of the democratic process, in the last analysis it is still one that is a healthier thing for the average person in the long run.

FROST: In other words, democracy has to be a bit frustrating and a bit inefficient?

LINDSAY: Again, go back to Mr. Churchill. He's the one that said it the best. He said, "Democracy is the very worst form of government ever devised by the mind of man except for every other form of government."

FROST: Looking back over your political career so far, what would you say is the most memorable phrase you've coined? Or created?

LINDSAY: I've coined or created? Very difficult. I wouldn't know. One that comes instantly to mind is when they asked me what my greatest accomplishment is as Mayor of New York City and I said "survival."

FROST: And how would you like to be remembered? I mean, how would you like the first line of your obituary in the *New York Times* to read?

LINDSAY: "Thanks so much."

FROST: If we were looking now at the political map of the world in ten years time, how would it look different than the way it does today?

LINDSAY: Well, you'll still have water between continents, and continents between water.

FROST: Even with the new TWA ads which say there is only a river in between.

LINDSAY: We'll have more water because we have not perfected the art of landfill as rapidly as water has discovered ways and means of shrinking the boundaries. But, I hope that we won't find the conditions when great huge chunks of the globe will be marked in one color saying this is one man's empire, and I don't think that's possible this day and age. We're in the age of decentralization, remember?

FROST: The Republican decentralization.

LINDSAY: And if we're going to decentralize the delivery of services in our cities by respecting the neighborhoods and communities, then, ergo, the world should do the same. Is that not true?

FROST: And the gospel of Republicanism should be spread throughout the world!

LINDSAY: Yes, that is correct, and let's go back to the urban problem because it's a global problem, very much so and maybe we'll come back to an age when civilization is marked by the health and condition of the cities of the world which was true at the time of Christ—immediately before and immediately thereafter—when empires kept rising and falling depending always on the condition of their metropolis.

Governor Nelson Rockefeller

DAVID FROST: In an election year, everyone behaves a bit like a doctor in the sense of trying to analyze what's wrong with the patient, as it were, America.

GOVERNOR NELSON ROCKEFELLER: You need to be a psychiatrist now!

FROST: Yes, exactly, because everybody talks about the malaise. What at root, if there is a malaise, would you say it is in America at the moment?

ROCKEFELLER: Well, I feel that the American people, perhaps for the first time, are beginning to lose confidence in themselves and in their country. I don't personally think it's justified. I think the problems that we face abroad and at home are not the weaknesses or the fault of the institutions, but the decisions that have been made by the leaders —and I'm not trying to be political about this—these decisions can be brought in tune with the problems of the times instead of being irrelevant to the problems of the times as they have been in many cases and that we can get back on the track and we can restore our confidence in ourselves and in our institutions. Now, you say, what are the principal questions. I think that the whole problem centering around Vietnam certainly is one of them, and this is reflected here. It's reflected around the world. I think the problem of our cities, where we've had these explosions from the ghetto areas, which of course have focused attention on a problem which has not been fully understood, fully recognized, or dealt with as it should have been. Those, I think, are the two most dramatic ones; I think there's a third that is just as serious and that is fiscal, monetary problems which are not being faced even yet and which are already, and could much more seriously in the future, undermine our strength and, frankly, they're not too dissimilar to some of the problems which you've had in your own country. We're following, I think very much in that same course, and I would hope that we can learn from some of the difficulties which you've had and try and correct them before we get—

FROST: We have managed to produce one or two mistakes for other people to learn from, I think.

ROCKEFELLER: Well, we've done plenty ourselves, and I didn't mean it in our sense, but they are really mistakes, largely of generosity of heart and wanting to do for people at home and abroad, more than we have the capacity to do. It's generosity, and this is a wonderful trait and a very worthy one, but it needs to be combined with realism or we undermine the very strength that makes it possible.

FROST: You were saying that the decisions have gone wrong on various issues, and you cited three. If we'd take one of them, let's say the cities and the ghettos, can you cite a decision you think should have gone differently? Or could have gone better?

ROCKEFELLER: Well, I would say first that I don't think that we have seen in perspective what was happening, that we've been going through not only an industrial revolution, but a revolution in the technology of agriculture, which perhaps is even more violent than the industrial revolution.

This has resulted in pushing off the land sharecroppers—this particularly talking now in terms of the South: sharecroppers, cotton pickers, tobacco pickers, who drifted through the urban areas finding no opportunity there. People with very little education, very little training, no cultural background in terms of the life that we understand today, and then who moved North seeking opportunity in the big city and well, let's take a case in point. We had three years ago, probably one of the first cities, a riot in Rochester. I got a call at 4:30 in the morning from the local officials saying things are out of hand, they lost control, would I send in the state police. We did. We were prepared. We'd trained them in riot control, and we took over at seven o'clock in the morning and got things back in hand, but what had happened was that here was probably one of the model cities in our country. There was two per cent unemployment and one of the most socially conscious, culturally advanced communities not only in our state, but in America. Yet they had a minority group population, primarily Negro, which they thought was around forty-five hundred. In ten years it had grown to over forty thousand come primarily from two counties, one in Florida and one in South Carolina. It had just grown overnight, and the community hadn't recognized what was happening and these people hadn't been absorbed. They were unskilled, primarily, with very little education, and the community hadn't adjusted to it. Now, this is in terms of both employment education and the deterioration of the physical environment in which they lived, all of which need to be dealt with positively. Now, the situation has exploded. We're now, I think, well, in this state at least, I hope taking the steps which will deal with this on a scale commensurate with the problems to remove the causes, but this is going to take a national commitment to do it on a national basis. However, the interesting thing is that this movement of people will be over. Minority groups from the rural South and rural Puerto Rico—within the next five to six years, this migration will have finished. It's already reduced tremendously, and maybe it's been—even though it's tough for the people themselves and for those who are sensing all the repercussions—maybe it's really a wonderful thing that they lived in a country that they could move around and where they could go to opportunity and where they can get education and training and good health and so forth. If we just move a little faster in dealing with these problems, it's going to turn out to have been constructive for all concerned.

FROST: Looking at all your career thus far, what's the one achievement you'd say you're most proud of?

ROCKEFELLER: Well, perhaps I'd say getting elected Governor and the opportunities afforded me to try and use the instrumentality of state government to solve problems in this federal system and to prove that the federal system does work today just as well as it did when it was conceived by the founding fathers.

FROST: Is there any incident that you'd like to rewrite? I mean, what was the worst moment thus far?

ROCKEFELLER: Well, I would suppose that taking a stand on the subject of extremism at the Republican convention four years ago and being roundly booed for fifteen minutes was a really interesting and valuable experience.

FROST: But as you stood there those fifteen minutes, you probably weren't thinking, "My, this is interesting and valuable."

ROCKEFELLER: Oh, I did, because I was given five minutes to make a speech. They postponed the time until it. was three o'clock in the morning in the East, so that it wouldn't have too much impact on the East as far as television was concerned, and they wanted to get me off and I said—look, I have five minutes, and my speech actually is four minutes and fifty seconds, so that I'm going to stay here all night. It's your responsibility if you can't control your own convention, but I'm going to deliver this message. I had been through an interesting campaign in California with bomb threats and calls, you know, something you really wouldn't sort of think in this country, and people who were supporting my campaign, women who were on committees run off the road at night, people breaking into their houses. It was a very interesting thing so that I felt pretty strongly about taking this position on extremism, although the position was certainly one that nobody could question; but the thing that really pleased me during the course of this was I felt that the audience was really making the point for me, that anybody who saw that program, could understand what I was talking about—partly by what I said, but more importantly by the response that convention was giving. I think their response did more to make the point than anything else. Now, politically it was unfortunate, but I think for the country it's better that we all see ourselves in perspective.

FROST: Yes, I saw it on television. It was a stunning experience. From the audio point of view, you obviously heard the noises. Were the audience demonstrating as well? Could you see them?

ROCKEFELLER: Oh yes. Shaking of fists, and they were really pretty sore. I don't blame them in a way because for quite a while, the conservative wing of the Republican Party had been frustrated in electing their candidates, and here was their chance and I had been through some primaries in which I had just analyzed the positions taken by Senator Goldwater. Now, I'm very fond of Senator Goldwater. He's an awfully nice person, but I think some of his positions were, let's say, not completely in tune with the times. By analyzing these and discussing them, it did make it difficult, I think, for him, so that there was quite a strong reaction at the convention.

FROST: At root, what would you say that people are on earth for?

ROCKEFELLER: Well, I could say this, that I think that if they want to get satisfaction out of life as individuals and enjoy happiness, that the greatest satisfaction they can get is by doing for others, is by contributing to the opportunity and full realization for people, small number, large number, within our country, within the world, and that the great satisfaction comes from that, and that the unique quality of the human being is his capacity to grow, to develop—to be able to recognize human and spiritual values, or spiritual human values, as distinct from animal.

FROST: Do you believe in the principle, "My country, right or wrong"?

ROCKEFELLER: It depends upon what position you're in. If you're a leader, you've got to put the emphasis on being right. If you're a citizen, I think you've got to support your country, hoping it's right.

FROST: But that allows for the fact that it may not be, obviously?

ROCKEFELLER: I mean, I'm sure that any leaders are going to make mistakes, but at this time, we can ill afford to make many because of the importance of the role that this country has in the world—and not only our responsibility to our own citizens, but to citizens of other countries.

FROST: As a leader, how would you define leadership? What should it be?

ROCKEFELLER: Well, the ability to determine through communications with people goals and objectives that are consistent with our heritage—in this country we've got a clear heritage—and then to find again in communications with people, common means of achieving those goals. Lincoln once said that the thing that had bound the federacy together was the common effort to lift the burdens from the shoulders of man, and this is a very interesting and a very exciting concept because, today, we really have that capacity in terms of modern society—to lift these burdens from the shoulders of man if we have the intelligence to use the forces which exist. I think we do, and this could be the factor that binds the world together, if we work together among nations to lift the burdens from the shoulders of man.

FROST: Looking back through history, which historical character do you most admire, or do you feel most in sympathy with?

ROCKEFELLER: I had the privilege and the unique opportunity of meeting on a number of occasions and having some quite lengthy conversations with Mahatma Gandhi back in 1930 or '31, and I had tremendous admiration and respect for him—conceptually, his approach and his feeling for life and for people and for values.

FROST: Someone was writing in *Life* magazine, I think it was this week, saying that because you're Rockefeller you therefore have the ability to move quickly and to be separate and so on from people and from people's budgets and spending at home. How do you conquer the problem of remoteness?

ROCKEFELLER: Of course I would challenge the statement of remoteness. First, it's a question of how you feel. Some people leave and go and try and find a place to be away because they don't like people and they want to be separate and apart from them. That's not true as far as I'm concerned. I'm very fond of people. I like people very much. I spend a great deal of time with people, whether it's just talking to them on the street, or over here on this construction job, or in the legislature, or wherever it happens to be, or campaigning of course. I don't know what your traditions are in campaigning. Probably they're similar to ours, but we do a great deal of campaigning on the street. I get a sound truck, and a group gathers and starts talking, sort of the old revival spirit. If you like people, it doesn't take long, in fact, maybe five or ten seconds to establish a sense of rapport.

FROST: In your campaigning, what was the most difficult heckle, most memorable remark, that someone you were meeting made to you?

ROCKEFELLER: Well, the hecklers, of course, in any audience liven up the scene tremendously, and if your wits are about you, you don't get pushed into a corner, and the audience enjoys it. If a person is disagreeable or unfair and you handle it with good grace, you know, in a friendly way, then they respond. I remember one time the first year I was campaigning for the nomination in '58, or having gotten the nomination, for the election as Governor, down in the lower east side in New York, and a lady said that she couldn't find a place to live within her means. Well, I was very filled with sympathy and I had studied the issues that were before the state, and I explained there were two bond issues, one for middle income housing of so many hundred million and another one for low income housing for so many hundred million and if she'd get her friends and get the support and with the right governor elected— and she looked up at me and said, "I should wait so long?" Well, I learned a great deal from that. As a matter of fact, I vowed right then and there that she wouldn't have to wait so long if I got elected Governor and as it turned out, it worked out correctly.

FROST: People think of you as someone who can really

get anything that you want, as it were, or afford things or whatever.

ROCKEFELLER: That's what they think.

FROST: Can you think of anything that you wanted that you weren't able to get?

ROCKEFELLER: Yes, in the field of art, it's been true. I remember bidding in an auction on a Modigliani once and losing to the Museum of Modern Art of which I then was president; and fourteen years later, another one came on the market and I was fortunate enough to get it, so it shows if you've got patience and persistence, even though you may be thwarted at one point, you can and I'm a great believer in that.

FROST: Again, this is a long way ahead, but how would you like to be remembered? What would you like the first line of your obituary in the *New York Times* to say?

ROCKEFELLER: That a few people were better off as a result of my having lived.

FROST: In an election year, everyone says that people are trying to find out what people are hoping for and what they're frightened of. What would you say this year is most Americans' main fear and most Americans' main hope?

ROCKEFELLER: Well, as I mentioned earlier, what worries me about this country is that they're beginning to lose confidence in themselves and in our country. I really feel that the United States does have—and the American people and their basic beliefs—a certain responsibility and a certain role to play that can be very important in terms of the future of the world. I'd like to see this country play that role, and they play it best when they're relaxed and confident, not boastful, but confident in their own capacity. I think this confidence needs to be restored. We talk about the decline of the Roman Empire, but other empires were coming forward. I think we're coming to a period and a sort of a crossroads where we could see possibly a decline of the structures of the world, the different nations, or we could come into the greatest period in the history of mankind; and it could go either way and very importantly in making that decision as to which way we're going to go, what this country does, what the American people do, or what their leaders do is going to make that determination, and I think it can go into the greatest period in the history of mankind.

FROST: I agree. I think that the world is in a situation at the moment where the mediocre guarantee has disappeared and we could go into a world of greater fulfillment or greater misery.

ROCKEFELLER: Exactly.

FROST: If there was one adjective about the way the Johnson Administration has been conducted that you wanted to get across to people more than any other, what would you pick?

ROCKEFELLER: Well, I think it's an administration that is dedicated to trying to do a good job, but that their concepts and actions are becoming less relevant to the realities of the world in which we live and therefore less effective.

FROST: And what is the basis of making one's actions as a politician relevant to the world we live in now?

ROCKEFELLER: Understanding the people who live in the world that we're in and the forces which govern and dominate what's happening.

Senator Robert F. Kennedy

DAVID FROST: Senator Kennedy, wherever I go in America, people always say to me this isn't the real America. If you had to pick one place, where would you point to and say that for you this was the real America?

SENATOR ROBERT F. KENNEDY: If you ask me for a specific place, I think perhaps smaller towns are. Upstate New York, Iowa, but I suppose there are a lot of different communities. I think once you get away from the large urban centers where life is a little bit more frantic, you might see more about the understanding and the courage and the compassion of people. You focus more upon it, I think, in some of our smaller communities.

FROST: In an election year, everyone behaves rather like a doctor, finding what's wrong with America and suggesting remedies. Do you think the things like the cities or the attitudes to the war or the race question are the malaise, or do you think they're symptoms of something deeper that's going to have to be put right?

KENNEDY: I think it's deeper. I think those are symptoms of it. I think it involves the national purpose and almost the soul of the country, and I think it involves also to some extent the tremendous material wealth we have in the United States and what you're going to do with it, how it's going to be utilized; also the tremendous military wealth or power that we have and the fact that we are involved in this terribly difficult struggle and we don't quite know what to make of it. I think it really comes down to the national purpose—what we're trying to accomplish and what is up at the top that's giving us some direction or some leadership.

FROST: You, more than anyone bidding for the Presidency, have a clearer conception of what the Presidency can do. Was there something that President Kennedy taught you about the scope of the Presidency? In a sense what you're saying is that it's got more potential than is being realized?

KENNEDY: I think that's true, and it goes beyond specific pieces of legislation. I think, you know, an awful lot of legislation can be passed, and you start arguing about what housing bill is better than another bill, or what job program or Manpower Training Program is better than another program, but people get lost with all of that, and understandably. They can't keep up with all of the things that are happening in their own community, let alone what is happening at the federal level, the legislation that is being passed. But the Presidency is something far beyond that. It's not that you're going to agree with the President on every issue. There's going to be tremendous disagreement, but the fact that it's giving the country some direction and there's somebody that you feel that's up there that's looking out for your own interest, not in a selfish way, and more beyond that the interest of the country and the interest of the next generation, though you might disagree with what he is doing, you can understand it and you rally to him and therefore to the country in time of crisis. For instance, President Kennedy's popularity was never higher than after the Bay of Pigs when he said we made a mistake but we've learned something from it. Although people thought that was a terrible disaster and a terrible mistake and wasn't he stupid and foolish to do it, you still honor the fact that whoever it is is part of you and part of your country and part of what you have such affection for.

FROST: That's what was exciting about the period '60 to '63. It seemed the first time that one person could set a style somehow, for a whole country.

KENNEDY: It's what the people are really. President Kennedy maybe stimulated it, but what made those days was not just—it wasn't him. He obviously played a role, but it was those young people who went and served, as I said. It was the young men and women who went and helped legislation. It was those who fought or struggled against discrimination, and it was people who were doing extra kinds of things on behalf of their neighbor or their community and felt that politics or political life was an honorable profession as John Buchan, Lord Tweedsmuir said, and that you can make a difference. So much now you are frustrated about the fact that you can't affect the course of action, or the course of events. You can't affect Vietnam. You can't affect the riots in the cities. You're white, and the blacks are going to try to come in and try to take your home away from you, are going to move into the neighborhood, or going to shoot somebody—and blacks the same about whites. Nobody's going to help, but it's a fact that somebody can make a difference, and it's worthwhile trying to make a difference.

FROST: Would your approach be similar to President Kennedy's?

KENNEDY: We're living in a different time. The late 1960's and the '70's are different than they were in the early 1960's. I was happy to be part of that, but that was part of my life that is past and what I'm looking to is not continuing what ended in 1963, but beginning what can happen in 1969 which will have an effect for the 1970's. That's what's important, not what we did in the early 1960's, but what we can do from now on.

FROST: What do you, Senator, as you look at your career thus far, feel proudest of, your greatest achievement thus far?

KENNEDY: I think the role in the Cuban Missile Crisis. I don't think there's anything else sort of compared to that. The only reason that I hesitated at all is because I felt strongly about the election of 1960 and having a role in the change, because I think that affected the course of action and the course of history at least for a period of time for the United States. Therefore having played a role in that was important, but if you took one event that I think was most important, most significant, and where I perhaps made the most contribution, where the question was whether the world is going to be blown up or not, that was the Cuban Missile Crisis.

FROST: And the contribution there, you said, was one of making the right decision or—

KENNEDY: The right decision was made by President Kennedy, but just the ideas that I was able to contribute on which he finally made—

FROST: If you become President, you've then got to find people like you, haven't you?

KENNEDY: Well, it's interesting because you see, if the fourteen people who were involved—who were very, very significant, bright, able, dedicated people, all who had the greatest affection for the United States, probably the brightest kind of group that you could get together under those circumstances—if six of them had been President of the United States, I think that the world might have been blown up. That's one side of it and the fact is, also—six out of fourteen—the other side of it is if Mr. Khrushchev had been a different man at that time, the world also would have blown up. When we think of how brilliant and able President Kennedy was, I think we have to also look at the other side of it—this also involves our adversaries. I think if you look back in history, or trace the evolvement of the first World War of Austria's miscalculation about what was going to happen and then the Soviet Union's miscalculation by calling up their troops and Germany's idea of— because Russia mobilized their troops, therefore they were going to take that step and then England taking and France reacting to that. Everybody involved in all of that miscalculated what the other person was going to do. Now you miscalculate in a major way, and that's the last miscalculation you make.

FROST: We all make jokes about our respective intelligence services, but in the last resort, the horror of getting wrong information today is there's not time to check it.

KENNEDY: Not only wrong information which is terribly important, but it's judgment. You can go back to the Cuban Missile Crisis—where are you going to intercept a particular vessel, where are you going to let that vessel go through? President Kennedy spent more time trying to give the Soviet Union time to calculate their position than to get the missiles out of Cuba. There was no question you could have brought it to a head at a much earlier time, and there were those involved in counseling President Kennedy who wanted to do it immediately. The idea of giving the other person time to understand what the consequences are is so important and to have some judgment about what he's going to do and will not do is so valuable. In the last analysis, if you ask me what the most important characteristic or what the most important qualification a person should have in that kind of a position it is judgment.

FROST: I can see very clearly why you picked Cuba. Is there any one episode in your career that you'd like to rewrite?

KENNEDY: An episode that's out of your hands or an episode that you can affect, or what?

FROST: The episode you can affect.

KENNEDY: I can't think of any immediately. Obviously there are things that are out of one's hands that I would rather had never occurred, but I don't know that there's anything that I think that I would have changed.

FROST: Nothing you wish you'd left unsaid or anything like that?

KENNEDY: I think that if—as President Eisenhower said about Richard Nixon when he was asked whether he could think of something he'd contributed—if you gave me a week, I could think of something. I'm sure I can think of a lot of things, and I'm sure there are things that I said in the last twenty-four hours that fill that category, but I think you're talking about in a major way. And during the course of my career—I mean obviously I made a lot of mistakes and—but if you're talking about in a major area in which I've had the control over the decisions I can't. I'm sure— perhaps if I thought about it, I probably could do it better.

FROST: We'll leave President Eisenhower and Richard Nixon to think about it. As you read about yourself in the press, do you recognize the picture of yourself, or is there something that we should know about you, some quality that you reckon doesn't get full play in the press?

KENNEDY: Kind, thoughtful, sweet—that kind of thing—

FROST: You think they miss a little.

KENNEDY: Occasionally. I don't know. I think that

117

they've had an opportunity to analyze me, so they can reach whatever conclusions perhaps much better than I can myself.

FROST: Everybody hopes they change and develop, but in your case, people particularly say that you've changed and developed. I read a book in which Ted Sorensen said how you changed. Do you feel you've changed more than most people?

KENNEDY: I don't know. I'm sure I've changed. I hope I've changed. I hope I've grown, and I hope I have more understanding and more comprehension and more compassion and all of those things that all of us would like to have as we grow older. I suppose up until November of 1963 that my whole life was built around President Kennedy. What was important to me and what I felt strongly about was not just the dedication to an individual and not a dedication to my brother, but just the fact that I thought through him that we could make a contribution and remedy injustices and change the direction of the United States and accomplish some good. So my life was dedicated to that, not so much as to what I was going to be or what role I was going to play or whether I was—the most beloved figure in the United States. I think that that was the only thing that meant anything to me. I expect after November, 1963, that perhaps I was looked upon with different eyes, and obviously I had to play a different role because what existed for me before that period of time didn't exist afterward.

FROST: People sort of felt that you had to do the unpopular things. You quoted '60 as one of the things you are proud of. You had to do the unpopular things in '60.

KENNEDY: Well, those people are my friends who excused me during those periods of time, "that's just because he has to do the unpopular things for his brother."

FROST: How would you define leadership?

KENNEDY: I think to inspire people to exercise their best qualities.

FROST: That's a pretty good definition.

KENNEDY: I was just thinking of that story about the French general who yelled out the window, "There go my people. I must follow them. I am their leader." I don't think that's it. I think it's the opposite of that.

FROST: Do you believe in the principle, "My country, right or wrong"?

KENNEDY: No, I think one has this affection or feeling for his country, but I think of what Camus said during the war with Algeria, that my criticism comes because I want to love my country in justice, and I think that's what we want. We want to have this affection and feeling for our country in justice.

FROST: Would you redefine today the word Communist? It doesn't mean the same as it did twenty years ago; it's not a monolithic international conspiracy any more, is it?

KENNEDY: No. I suppose there's a difference in each one of the countries really. I mean, I suppose one of the reasons that it's less dangerous and why we have to adjust ourselves about it is it's not just a system that's controlled out of one nation's capital and therefore the kind of power that it was before. I think it's very difficult because I suppose there's as much difference between what is happening in China and what is happening in Czechoslovakia today as between what is happening in the United States and happening in a country in Latin America. When you say the United States and Indonesia are democracies and Peru and Brazil, how do you define democracy? The country adapts to a social and political system which evolves to something that is either satisfactory to the people or satisfactory to those that are presently in power.

FROST: What frightens me a bit is the way in which people will dub a nation or someone a Communist, without really being able to define the word.

KENNEDY: I think probably that's one of the struggles between the young and the older generation because here in the United States the older generation, and quite rightly, thinks of Communism. If you went up until 1960 you'd think of what they did right after the war. You think of Stalin, and you think of the rape of Hungary. You think of the sweep across Europe. You think of the Korean War —all of these incidents that occurred which showed them the bitterest and most difficult kinds of enemies. Then along came President Kennedy who talked about lowering the barriers and that we have to try to have an accommodation with our adversaries and then the test ban treaty. The younger generation came on the world scene during that period of time, not having lived through any of these other events and so they think of Communism as being in some cases a terrible system and in other parts of the world, nothing much worse than some of our allies. The older generation think back on all of these events and say how can you trust a Communist or how can you ever accept the idea that there should be a Communist. Therefore, when we talk in our own country of the struggle between the young and the old, I think part of it at least is due to that. I think also it's economic problems, but I think at least part of it is due to that; but when you asked me the question, I think it's whether you're talking about Rumania, Czechoslovakia, the Soviet Union, or China. That's very, very difficult. I think that the fundamental concern about it really is the fact that up to the present time, when there are so many countries that are in transition, the individual did not play the role that he should play and there was control by the state over the individual. The individual existed on behalf of the state and with a dictatorship which was unsatisfactory.

FROST: You were talking about recent history. Looking back through history, which historical character do you feel most in sympathy with? That you most admire?

KENNEDY: There are some marvelous romantic brave figures, whether it was James Cook, or the Swamp Fox, but I think from a political point of view, Abraham Lincoln. Let's see—well, most of the ones that I really think about rapidly are Americans, but I think probably Abraham Lincoln. Theodore Roosevelt I admire a great deal. I admired a lot in Herbert Hoover's career. I thought his earlier career, and what he did working in the mines, his career in China, what he did for Europe after the first World War and what he did during the 1950's, the Hoover Commission in the United States, marvelous contributions to our country and to his fellow man. Of course he had difficulties in the 1920's as part of the cabinet and then while he was President of the United States, but when you consider his overall career, there are some marvelous things that he did. Another person whom I admired is Charles Lindbergh.

FROST: As a pioneer?

KENNEDY: I thought he was brave and courageous, independent, and a lot of characteristics.

FROST: You're often pictured in the open air. Some people write about you as if you're reckless and—

KENNEDY: Ruthless?

FROST: No, well—ruthless too. We'll come to ruthless, but I was only saying reckless! You just heard ruthless.

KENNEDY: Oh, that's what I hear so much.

FROST: No, reckless in the sense of all the physical things you do. Other people say you're very cautious.

121

Which of the two portraits do you recognize the most? Are you sometimes reckless?

KENNEDY: No, I don't think I'm reckless.

FROST: But you like physical risk, don't you?

KENNEDY: Well, I enjoy doing some of those kinds of things. Edith Hamilton wrote that men are not made for safe havens. That's part of a human being's life, or a man's life.

FROST: What about the other word you heard, the ruthless—why do people say that?

KENNEDY: I don't know. I'm sure you're going to get a lot of people to explain exactly why. I can't tell you. I think that's a difficult point for me to answer. I mean, why do you beat your wife?

FROST: I suppose you'd rephrase it as decisive.

KENNEDY: No, I wouldn't try. They're entitled to what they think.

FROST: What would you say, at root, that people are on earth for?

KENNEDY: I think you'd probably break it down to people who have some advantages and those who are just trying to survive and have their family survive. If you have enough to eat, for instance, I think basically it's to make a contribution to some of us who are less well off. "I complained because I had no shoes until I met a man who had no feet." You can always find someone that has a more difficult time than you do, has suffered more, and has faced some more difficult time one way or another. If you've made some contribution to someone else, to improve their life, and make their life a little bit more livable, a little bit more happy, I think that that's what you should be doing.

FROST: How would you like to be remembered? What would you like the first line of your obituary to say?

KENNEDY: Something about the fact that I made some

contribution to either my country or those who are less well off. I think again back to what Camus wrote about the fact that perhaps this world is a world in which children suffer, but we can lessen the number of suffering children, and if you do not do this, then who will do this. I'd like to feel that I'd done something to lessen that suffering.

FROST: Some people define an election year as a year in which people are trying to find out what the electorate are hoping for and what they're frightened of. What would you say is most Americans' main fear and main hope at this moment?

KENNEDY: It's a hope for a national purpose. That sounds general, but I really think that's what it is fundamentally, the end of divisions within the country; not the end, because we can never end them, but I mean, to escape from the bitterness and the hatred that exists to a greater extent in the United States than perhaps it has for a number of generations and to give us some national purpose and restore the soul to the country. What was the other question?

FROST: The fear.

KENNEDY: The fear that we won't.

FROST: National purpose is another thing that's terribly difficult to define.

KENNEDY: I know, and perhaps everybody uses it. I think it's true, however. I mean, I don't want to sound like sort of a speech that one gives on a patriotic holiday, but I think more than for instance in 1960 there is what President Johnson in his State of the Union Message called restlessness, and Secretary Gardner talked about the fact that people felt lost and that the sense of action had gone out of people. We have this tremendous gross national product. We have this tremendous wealth, the economy is going up fantastically high. The individual is making much more money and what does it all mean once we have it? If children and parents are becoming alienated from one another, if there's greater bitterness between blacks and whites, as there is now, and we're very bitter over the war in Vietnam, then you wonder just what direction you're going in and what this all means. I just think we can do much, much better in this country and that we've done such marvelous things. I just think that we can do much, much better, and I don't want to continue like we have over the period of the last five years. I don't believe that the American people do. I think we want to turn a corner, and I don't think we can at the moment.

FROST: Do you feel at the moment that in this campaign that you're waging now your family name is a tremendous advantage.

KENNEDY: Yes.

FROST: Is there any ways in which it's ever hindered what you've been trying to do?

KENNEDY: No, I think it focuses more attention on what I say and what I did before I became a candidate, and therefore there's more controversy about what I do and what I say. Somebody else could say it, and there's not a great deal of criticism. If I get involved in it, I pay some price for it, but obviously it's a great asset because I think people have such great affection for President Kennedy.

FROST: Do you ever worry about how your children are ever going to be able to feel that they've in any way topped what you've done?

KENNEDY: No, I think that they'll develop their own lives. I talked to one of my sons about it at one time. We were talking about what he was going to do, and he said—

he was twelve years old—he wanted to make a contribution. He said "I didn't want to get involved in political life." And I said, "Well, what do you want to do?" He said, "I want to make a contribution." He loves animals, and he knows all about them and has read about them, and he said, "I want to make a contribution like Darwin and Audubon did." I think people work out their own lives. He wants to make that kind of contribution, and I think the other ones will do the same thing, just as long as they understand that in the last analysis, what is important is that they give something to others and not just turn in on themselves and decide that they are important. What they can contribute is the only thing that matters.

FROST: It would be quite difficult for them to find a higher office than, say, the Presidency of the United States to move on to, but you think they're going to move on to separate fields?

KENNEDY: Well, I suppose, but they're young, and I would hope that they would adjust. Whatever that means!

FROST: If you weren't in politics, what would you be doing now?

KENNEDY: I think I'd probably like to teach. I'd like to go to a university and perhaps like to read more and perhaps write.

FROST: Looking at the United States in ten years time if we could do it tonight, how would you say it would look different and be different from what it is today.

KENNEDY: Well, what would I like to see the United States be, or what do I think it's going to be—

FROST: What do you think it's going to be?

KENNEDY: Areas in which I think we really have to accomplish something are that we've made a major contribution in trying to cut down in the reliance on nuclear weapons, that we've taken steps toward disarmament, that we've developed a system along with other nations of the world to help the underdeveloped nations of the world, and that we've established a system within our own country so that people can—even the very poor and the impoverished—educate their children so that they in turn could find decent jobs and live a decent life and not be hopeless and not be filled with despair. That's what I'd like to see.

FROST: And do you think these goals are obtainable?

KENNEDY: Yes. We can make some progress toward them, and we should try and that's what I think it's all about. That's why I think if we don't start trying in 1969, that we're going to start running out of time because, if we have the capacity to destroy all mankind, we have to start making some progress.